The
Drinking Man's Diet
COOKBOOK

Under the editorial direction of
ROBERT W. CAMERON
with the cooperation of a panel of
doctors, nutritionists, and home economists

CAMERON AND COMPANY, San Francisco, California

Acknowledgments

This book would not have been possible without the encouragement of a pioneer in nutrition, Dr. Agnes Faye Morgan, of the University of California. Her insight into the need for about 60 grams of carbohydrates a day sets this book apart from the many copycats in the dietary field. The basic idea for The Drinking Man's Diet originated with Jeffreys Corner. In the preparation of this updated version of the 1967 classic, special thanks go to Linda Henry for production expertise, Michi Toki for design, and Robert Burger for editing.

CAMERON AND COMPANY

680 EIGHTH ST., SUITE 205 SAN FRANCISCO, CA 94103

800 779 5582 abovebooks.com

© 2007 Cameron & Company, San Francisco

Library of Congress Control Number: 2007930965

The Drinking Man's Diet Cookbook 0-918684-63-3

Manufactured in the United States of America

TABLE OF CONTENTS

INTRODUCTION
THE DIET THAT INSPIRED
THIS BOOK...

It's a foregone conclusion that people drink. The Gallup Poll reported in 2006 that 192 million Americans have at least an occasional drink each week. Introduced in 1964, the Drinking Man's Diet was based on that reality, was an instant success and has sold 2,400,000 copies to date.

Many of those successful dieters asked for a follow-up book to provide low-carbohydrate recipes and menus without having to do a lot of arithmetic. That book was published in 1967 and was a Literary Guild selection. And here, forty years later, is an update of that cookbook, which includes all the features of the original diet plan, also updated!

The premise of this remarkable diet is that calories may count but there are several different kinds of calories. Some calories have low satiety value, and these are generally carbohydrates. The calories recommended by the Drinking Man's Diet are low in carbohydrates and high in satiety. But you *must* have carbohydrates in your diet, a minimum of 60 grams for good health. So this diet goes one step further and separates the carbohydrates into those that are especially good for you in nutrient value and those that are less so.

Unlike later low-carbohydrate diets, notably the Atkins plan, this diet had the nutrition right from the very beginning. Here's how it happened:

Years ago the U.S. Air Force was facing a growing problem of weight among its pilots on extended training flights. They were bored, and so they took to snacking on the usual carbohydrate culprits, sugary foods and starches. The Air Force looked into the matter and found a diet that worked for their young men. When I chanced upon it, I realized that many of my friends who had cocktails before dinner or wine during meals also, like those bored pilots, tended to eat the "culprit" carbohydrates to excess. The hors d'oeuvres, the desserts, the potatoes and bread in between.... So I decided to call this the "Drinking Man's Diet."

Before publishing it, however, I needed to have scientific evidence to show how it worked and why it was healthful. I called on Agnes Faye Morgan, Professor Emeritus and former head of the Department of Nutritional Sciences at the University of California, Berkeley. When I phoned her, I asked how I would find her office. She answered, "Ask the gatekeeper to direct you to Agnes Faye Morgan Hall."

When I explained my story, this slender, well-groomed lady leaned back in her chair and said, "Mr. Cameron, I've been on the Drinking Man's Diet for fifty years." Then she explained it to me: "Carbs store fat. If you cut back on them, you're going to cut back on fat. But remember this: if you don't get about 60 grams of carbohydrate a day, you'll have an unpleasant condition called ketosis. And without the *right kinds* of carbohydrates, namely the green leafy vegetables, you'll miss out on important nutrients."

That was enough for me. And after more than forty years of success, this diet continues to gather medical evidence that *this careful scrutiny of carbohydrates in your diet* makes eminent sense.

And, once again, the cookbook based on that diet makes good sense. There are more than 200 recipes here that have been carefully planned so that, instead of counting the carbohydrates in one food after another, all you have to do is look at a recipe or a full dinner menu as a whole. The work has been done for you. We even suggest wine selections for the main courses.

You'll also be happy to know that this is a cookbook that can easily stand on its own as an all-purpose, health-conscious guide to good dining. The team of food professionals who produced these well-organized menus included two food editors from the leading popular magazine of the West. I would love to give them all credit, but their work speaks for itself. Their emphasize on fresh, natural ingredients and simplicity of preparation foreshadowed what we now know as "California cuisine." You will enjoy what they have laid out before you as much as what they have done for your well-being and for your waistline!

Robert Cameron
July 2007

1
APPETIZERS
THAT CHECK THE CARBS

The cocktail hour can easily become a dietary downfall. Let's look at it realistically—from the standpoint of carbohydrates. When you're on the Drinking Man's Diet you know that almost all pre-dinner drinks, such as gin, vodka, scotch, bourbon, and dry white wine, are carbohydrate-free. The problem is what is served with them.

Let's start with those go-alongs that are put in front of you. In every one of those potato chips, sitting innocently by the bowl of 'dunk', a gram of carbohydrate is lurking. And just one square cracker or toast round can add 3 grams of carbohydrate, before you help yourself to another. No computer is needed to tell you that in three or four trips to the 'dunk' bowl those chips and crackers alone—not counting the 'dunk'—can cut deeply into your allowance of 60 grams per day.

Better bets for cocktail time are protein items, let's call them 'protein pickups' that can be speared with toothpicks: cubes of cheese, tiny meatballs, smoked salmon, shrimp. There's scarcely a carb in half a dozen helpings.

When you are the host, try serving an assortment of these 'protein pickups' as appetizers, along with fresh veggies such as short lengths of celery, broccoli flowerets, and green, red, or yellow peppers. Any number of simple dips go well with these, from humus to pesto to salsa. Guacamole has become the official dip of sporting events. Bottom line: the raw veggies have some carbs, but are a great trade-off in their nutritional value.

Now let's consider some old-time favorites that fit the diet, all of which can be prepared in advance and refrigerated, to be set out when guests arrive.

Egg balls

- 2 hard-boiled eggs
- 2 teaspoons prepared mustard
  dash, curry powder
  dash, seasoned salt
- 1 cup grated Cheddar cheese

Chop eggs. Mix with all seasonings. Spread a level of cheese on waxed paper. Spoon small balls of mixture one at a time onto cheese and roll thoroughly, about 16 balls in all. To serve, set each ball on a chip or cracker.

Carbohydrates: mainly in the chips or crackers!

Shellfish tidbits

- 1 cup diced shellfish, fresh, frozen, or canned (shrimp, crab, calamari, clams)
  Jalapena or green taco sauce
  Fresh lemon or lime juice

Slice shellfish into small pieces and set toothpick in each. Chill. Reserve fish juices to add to sauce when ready to serve. Season to taste and preserve freshness by squeezing lime or lemon over when served.

Carbohydrates: virtually none

Pickled eggs

A surprising appetizer for an outdoor barbecue featuring salmon. Note these require planning: two days!

- 1 dozen eggs, hard boiled and shelled
- 2 cups cider vinegar
- 2 tablespoons sugar
- 1 teaspoon salt
- 1 teaspoon mixed pickling spices (thyme, rosemary, dill, etc.)
  Diced garlic and onion, sprig of dill if available

Pack the eggs into quart jars, simmer mixture for a few minutes. Pour hot over eggs in jars. Cover and let stand in refrigerator for two days. Serve icy cold, either whole or cut into halves.

Carbohydrates: virtually none

Olive tricks

Here are two other "advanced preparation" appetizers, to be kept in refrigerator for a day or longer. This works in your favor!

First:
Bottle, stuffed olives
½ **cup, Roquefort or blue cheese**
¼ **cup, mayonnaise**
¼ **cup, finely chopped pecans or walnuts**

Mix mayonnaise and cheese to create malleable paste. Forcefully roll olives in paste, then in chopped nuts. Set on covered plate in refrigerator until needed.

Second:
Bottle or can , whole ripe olives
2 **cloves, sliced fresh garlic**
¼ **lemon, sliced**
1 **cup olive oil**

Drain olives and place in container (plastic, jar) that barely covers. Add all mixture and close tightly. Save in refrigerator until needed. Garnish with parsley in serving. (Retain olive oil mixture for use in salads.)

Carbohydrates: 1 gram per 5 olives

Salami cones

1 **dozen salami slices**
1 **dozen cubes Provolone cheese**
Dijon mustard to dot cheese
Alternate: substitute cubes of cantaloupe for cheese and mustard

Use toothpicks to secure salami wrapped around either cheese or cantaloupe. Serve over lettuce.

Carbohydrates: none

Sherry special

2 ounces, packaged turkey slices
4 slices Swiss cheese, quartered
 Dijon mustard to taste
 Dill weed

When a dry sherry is your cocktail, match it with these pungent accompaniments. Roll cheese and turkey together or simply serve separately, with carrot slivers.

Carbohydrates: only in the sherry, about 2 per glass

Celery snap-ups

3 oz. cream cheese
2 tablespoons bouillon or equivalent stock
2 tablespoons each: chopped green onions, parsley, green pepper, carrots, chives
 Worcestershire sauce to taste, and salt/pepper
1 dozen celery sticks, short lengths from center stalk

Mix stuffing thoroughly, in advance if desired, then fill celery stalks just before serving, to maintain crispness.

Carbohydrates: 1 gram per stalk, plus slight amount from stuffing

Pickled salmon or tuna

Here canned seafood works well, as the pickling provides the dominant flavor. Note: this requires two days storage.

1 can, salmon or tuna (6-7 ounces)
1 scallion (green onion), finely chopped
1 teaspoon coarse black pepper
1 teaspoon, chopped hot red peppers (chile tepins) or equal
1 cup vinegar

Flake, but do not dice, fish. Stir together all ingredients except vinegar. Place in shallow container so that vinegar will cover. Store in refrigerator, covered, until ready to serve. Serve on toasted bread wedges or, with small forks, over lettuce on appetizer plates.

Carbohydrates: only in bread wedges

Frosted ham cake

- 1   small can deviled ham
- ½   cup, cream cheese
- 1   teaspoon mayonnaise
- 1   bowl salted crackers

A quick dip: simply empty deviled ham on small plate, keeping as intact as possible. Whip cream cheese and mayonnaise together and 'frost' over ham.

Carbohydrates: only in the crackers

Artichoke leaves

- 2   large artichokes, cooked (p. 78)
-    Dash, Worchester sauce
- ½   lemon
- ½   cup, mayonnaise
-    Dash, dry mustard (such as Coleman's)
- 1   tablespoon, grated Parmesan cheese

Combine sauce ingredients in advance and let rest in refrigerator. When artichokes are still warm from steaming, discard layer of stiff outer leaves and pull off as many remaining leaves as needed for serving. Arrange on small plates around mound of sauce in middle, for dipping. Save remaining leaves and hearts for salad another day!

Carbohydrates: 1 gram per dozen leaves

Cheese block

1	3-oz. package cream cheese
¼	cup butter
3	tablespoons sesame seeds
1	medium cucumber
1	small bowl corn chips

Preparation is truly simple: toast sesame seeds in skillet for just a minute or so, take up, then quickly brown butter. Set chilled cream cheese in its original oblong shape on a small plate. Pour butter over it and sprinkle with seeds. Serve on thinly sliced cucumber, using small knife, or allow guests to scoop up with firm corn chips.

Carbohydrate: few in chips, little in cucumber

Baby lobster or prawns

Availability varies for these wonderful crustaceans. Choose what's local.

- **2** tablespoons sesame seeds
- **¼** cup soy sauce
- **½** lemon or seasoned rice vinegar
- **6** cooked baby lobster, prawns, or large shrimp

If necessary, slice lobster or prawns into bite-sized pieces and chill. Arrange on plate around sauce mix. These are just right for the first martini!

Three all-time favorites

Here are bite-sized hors d'oeurves for that special occasion. Surprisingly, they are so simple they can each be explained in a sentence, and so low in carbohydrates that no count is needed.

First: **Dried beef horseradish rolls.** Mix soft cream cheese with prepared horseradish and spread on slices of dried beef. Roll them up and chill. Slice into smaller pieces, pierce with cocktail picks, and serve on watercress or butter lettuce.

Second: **Avocado with bacon crumbles.** Mash ripe avocado and mix with crumbled bacon, seasoning with lemon and pepper. Serve on cucumber slices with a dash of paprika.

Third: **Caviar-stuffed eggs.** Prepare deviled eggs (p. 73) to meet your needs. The difference: make a slight depression in each half and fill with caviar.

Vienna Sausage Vino

- **1** nine-oz. can Vienna sausages
- **1** three-oz. can white mushrooms, or six fresh mushrooms, cooked and sliced
  Dash of herbs: thyme, marjoram, oregano
- **½** cup thinly sliced red onion
- **1** cup hearty red wine, such as syrah or zinfandel

Drain sausages, cut in half, and combine with herbs, onion, and mushrooms. Heat gently in skillet, gradually adding wine. Serve in chafing dish with cocktail picks.

Carbohydrates: virtually none

Browned pork tidbits Hawaiian

1   lb. lean pork loin
1   cup canned pineapple in sauce
½   cup herbs, such as cilantro, dill, scallions

Cut pork loin into small cubes, ½ inch square and marinate in sauce from canned pineapple, along with herbs.

Bake in 350 degree oven for 30 minutes, turning occasionally. Meanwhile, slice pineapple into wedges of similar size. Allow pork to rest for 15 minutes, then spear them to pineapple with cocktail picks. Return to warm oven, if necessary, if serving is delayed. Serve warm.

Carbohydrates: 1 per wedge of pineapple

Meatballs and ham

Allow at least four hours for advance preparation.

1   lb. lean ground beef
1   can (4-½ oz) deviled ham, or equivalent
20   small bits of blue cheese
1   cup dry red wine
1   teaspoon butter
1   teaspoon olive oil

Mix meats together, seasoning with salt and pepper. Form them around blue cheese bits into small meatballs. Marinate in wine in refrigerator for three hours.

Twenty minutes before serving, brown in skillet with butter and oil, in several batches to allow separation. Place in casserole dish and keep in 300 degree oven until ready to serve, basting with balance of red wine as needed.

Optional: add finely chopped onion to original beef mixture.

Carbohydrates: 1-2 per meatball

Another skillet special: blazing meatballs

Put on a show with an ordinary appetizer: bring on the brandy. Use the above meatballs or canned/frozen variety, without sauce. Brown in a little butter, then ladle in a jigger of brandy. When ready to serve, light with a match and bring on blazing! Serve with cocktail picks as before.

Back to dips: the secret

Cheese adds very little to carbohydrates and a lot to the foundation of any appetizer recipe. A soft cheese, or a hard cheese grated; a mild cheese or a Stilton. Mix your cheeses, but never be bland. Then try any number of ingredients:

Anchovies, minced clams, shrimp
Onion soup mix, avocado mix, chili peppers, olives
Gin, vodka, whiskey, scotch, table wine, sherry, port

And the fresh herbs: cilantro, garlic, dill weed, leek. Experiment with them all, tasting as you go.

Ideas for barbecue appetizers

Barbecue has become so much a part of our lives that we may overlook how it can be used for starters. When the backyard or patio barbecue is chicken or ribs, why not think big and broil a small, thin strip of top sirloin as an appetizer?

Or shrimp on skewers? Or sea scallops? Or simply mushrooms and red/green peppers.

A cheese fondue can be kept bubbling on the side of the grill in a small skillet—just enough to keep the chef out of the kitchen, and on the job: watching his coals.

2
SEAFOOD
FOR SOUL AND BODY

Fish of all kinds has become prominent in a healthful diet because of a certain fish oil, omega-3 fatty acids, which reduces triglycerides in the blood. The omega-3 revolution plays a big role in healthier hearts. Cold-water fish such as salmon, mackerel, and herring are especially high in omega-3s. But tuna, sole, flounder, cod, and shellfish also contribute. And seafood is also a smart choice because of what it *replaces:* the saturated fat of red meat. From the very beginning, the Drinking Man's Diet has taken health into account in food choices. This is why it has always been more than a fad.

Like practically all meats, seafood is high in protein and very low or lacking in carbohydrates. And you never have to trim away fat from fish – an important distinction from meats.

The best way to manage the preparation of any meal built around broiled, sautéed, or steamed fish is to have everything else ready before you start to cook the fish. The advice of chefs is "Fish fillets or slices should be cooked last, cooked fast, and served immediately on very hot plates."

Cooking fish in the oven has two advantages: It doesn't require close watching, and your guests will be unaware that fish is being cooked. Yet always remember: fish can easily be over-cooked. When you're doing fairly thin slices, steaks, or fillets, you can watch and turn them carefully in the pan. But when you're doing a whole or thick piece of fish in the oven it's wise to use a meat thermometer. The fish is done at 140 degrees – never more than that. Experienced cooks say "If you can smell fish cooking, it's already over-done." Dinner has been ruined!

Broiling fish without turning: simplicity itself!

Fillets or steaks are easier to do and attractive to serve when they are broiled this simple way.

Wipe fish dry with paper towel and sprinkle with salt. Line a shallow baking or broiling pan with foil (don't place fish on a rack). Oil or butter foil. Turn broiler to preheat so oven will also be hot.

Heat an over-proof pan on range, so that fish will begin cooking from bottom as well as top. Put fish in pan, fillets skin-side down. (You may remove skins after cooking.) Coat fish with butter and place under broiler, 2-4 inches from flame depending on thickness of fish. Adjust rack under pan as needed, and use low rather than high broil. The fish will brown quickly. Test with fork for flakiness. Turn off broiler and leave fish in hot oven a short time if not done throughout.

Serve with sprinkles of parsley on plates warmed in oven.

No carbohydrates

The Perfect Veggie and Fish Combo

Here's a simple change of pace from overly complex meals, based on the broiled fish above: Start by steaming new or red potatoes and your favorite vegetable (spinach, green beans, broccoli, summer squash) until near done. Prepare fish as above, adding potatoes cut into halves and buttered, under broiler with fish.

Serve hot or jellied consommé as appetizer, along with carrot or cucumber sticks, as you prefer. Add lemon wedges for fish.

A simple dry white wine completes the picture.

Carbohydrates: in the vegetables—consult tables

Fillet of sole in white wine sauce

For four persons, select 4 large or 8 medium fillets of sole, or petrale, flounder, sand dabs, English sole or similar small white fish. Salt and pepper them. In a large skillet, combine the following:

- **2 tablespoons butter**
- **1 teaspoon chopped green onion**
- **1 teaspoon chopped parsley**
- **2 or 3 mushrooms, sliced**
- **1 stalk celery, chopped**

Sauté for a few minutes, then add:

- **1 bay leaf**
- **1 cup dry white wine**
- **½ cup consommé (or fish stock)**

When liquids simmer, add fillets, a few at a time, and let simmer for a few minutes until just tender. If there are skins, remove them at this time, and, using a spatula, assemble fillets in an ovenproof platter or baking dish.

Next, reduce the liquid in the skillet under moderate heat until about ¾ cup remains, and add:

- **2 tablespoons heavy cream**

and strain over fish in platter. Sprinkle heavily with Parmesan cheese.

At this point you can cover and save the platter in the refrigerator, for finishing later. This is why it's a good "company" main dish. When it's time to finish, about 10 minutes before serving, heat oven to 400 degrees and bake until lightly browned.

Carbohydrates: about one gram per serving

Suggested wine: Vouvray or Sauvignon Blanc

Salmon or halibut baked with sour cream

Ask your seafood purveyor for a large fish body, 2 to 2½ lb., that is, from the head portion of a fillet that will be about an inch thick. Wash thoroughly and marinate for an hour or two in white wine or soy sauce, with any mixture of onions, garlic, and herbs of your preference.

Rinse when ready to cook, place in a buttered baking pan, and cover with:

1 **cup sour cream**
1 **teaspoon salt (not necessary if you have used soy sauce in the marinade)**
   ground or seasoned pepper to taste
   onions, garlic and other herbs removed from marinade

Bake at 375 degrees for about 20 minutes, or until it flakes when tested with a fork. Remember: you can always cook more, but you can't uncook.

Carbohydrates: about 2 grams per serving

Suggested wine: Chardonnay

Combining baked fish with accompaniments for a full dinner

Start with the salmon or halibut fillet recipe above—any other large fish will also work. Parboil new (or red) potatoes in advance, and add halves to the fish baking pan. Prepare also in advance a cabbage salad (p. 102). Offer a sampling of cheeses for dessert.

Going easy on the potatoes, a guest will have fewer than 20 carbohydrates for the entire dinner. A light red wine can easily work with the main course and the dessert. The richness of the baked fish and the cabbage can take it!

Baked halibut platter

Here's a simple alternative to the baked halibut or salmon with sour cream, above. Begin with steaks rather than fillets. Trim skin, separate center bones out. Then cut remaining fish into serving-size pieces. You'll need, for four servings:

2   lbs. halibut steak, about 1 inch thick
2   tablespoons lemon juice
1   teaspoon grated onion
3   tablespoons melted butter

Mix lemon juice, onion, and butter in a shallow bowl and dip fish pieces into it, with salt and pepper to taste. Place fish on platter or baking pan, cover with any remaining liquid, and bake in preheated oven at 350 degrees until tender enough to flake under a fork. Don't overcook! Sprinkle with parsley and paprika to serve.

Carbohydrates: fewer than 3 grams total

Broiled mountain trout

Your seafood merchant may offer trout whole or cleaned and filleted. If the former, clean, remove head, tail, and fins, trimming generously all around. Wash thoroughly after trimming is complete, then brush with butter, salt and pepper Trout will cook quite quickly under a low broil—a few minutes. Again, test with a fork so as not to overcook.

Carbohydrates: none

Vacation breakfast

Broiled trout, as above, with Canadian bacon slowly fried stove-top. Shirred eggs in tomatoes (p. 69). Buttered toast with sour cream.

Now this is a vacation! Going easy on the toast, there's no more than 11 carbohydrates here, and it smacks of the great outdoors.

Poached fillets of sole with salmon

Here's an interesting combination of delicate white fish with flavorful red salmon, both poached, then served with a cream sauce—a recipe from Holland. For four:

8	medium fillets of sole or flounder
½	lb. Salmon fillet
	salt and pepper
1	tablespoon vinegar or lemon juice
1	small bay leaf
	slice of onion
	dill weed
2	tablespoons butter
2	tablespoons flour
1⅓	cups fish stock
⅓	cup dry white wine
⅓	cup heavy cream
1	egg yolk, beaten
2	tablespoons capers (or chopped chives)
2	tablespoons chopped parsley

If sole is frozen, defrost completely so pieces can be rolled up. Sprinkle each fillet lightly with salt and pepper and dill weed. Cut salmon into 8 strips, removing bones and skin. Place a piece of salmon at large end of sole fillet, roll up, and secure with toothpick. Boil salted water in skillet or saucepan, sufficient to cover roll-ups, add bay leaf and onion slice, and roll-ups without crowding.

Poach (simmer) for 5-6 minutes, or until fish flakes when tested with a fork. Be sure not to overcook or roll-ups will begin to fall apart.

Carefully lift roll-ups from skillet, remove toothpicks, and place in a platter or casserole dish in a 250 degree oven. Empty skillet.

Now make a thin cream sauce in skillet: melt butter, add flour, and cook, stirring constantly, for two minutes or less. Add fish stock and wine to mixture, stirring under medium-low heat until it all thickens smoothly—about four minutes. Stir in cream and beaten egg, and continue cooking for no more than two minutes. Remember: there's nothing worse than egg yolk that cooks before fully mixed.

When ready to serve, pour cream sauce over fish and sprinkle with capers, chives, or parsley.

Carbohydrates: about 4 grams per serving

Suggested wine: Chardonnay or Gewürztraminer

Curried Seafood

This is an ambitious and rich dinner in itself, which can be served over rice and with vegetables as desired. It can be prepared as a sauce in advance, without the seafood until ready to be served, and this also enhances the curry flavor.

- 2 tablespoons butter
- 2 scallions (green onions), chopped (tops and all)
- 1 small clove garlic
- 4 tablespoons cornstarch
- 2 tablespoons curry powder (you may also use the main ingredients of curry powder—cardoman, cumin)
- ½ cup consommé, chicken broth, or milk
- 1 cup light cream

This completes the pre-preparation ingredients. Then:

- 1 tablespoon chutney
- 2 tablespoons lemon juice
- 1 or 1½ cups fresh cooked or canned crab meat, or crab in shells
- 1 or 1½ cups fresh cooked or pre-cooked shrimp in shells

Prepare the sauce by cooking onion and garlic over low heat in butter, without browning, Discard garlic, blend in cornstarch and curry powder, stir in cornstarch and cream and cook while stirring until smoothly thickened. You may now refrigerate.

When ready to serve, add chutney, lemon juice, crab, and shrimp (deveined). Heat slowly on low, season to taste when hot but not boiling.

The usual accompaniments include chutney and any chopped nuts; more imaginative are crumbled crisp bacon, finely chopped hard-boiled egg, shredded fresh coconut, chopped preserved ginger, or tiny pickled onions.

You may substitute other shellfish as desired: Alaskan king crab, lobster, lobster tails, scallops, salad shrimp. Shrimp and crab in shells generally work best because they blend in more easily with the sauce.

Carbohydrate: about 30 grams for entire recipe, not including rice

Suggested wines: full-bodied chardonnay, Beaujolais

Salmon loaf or cakes, Crab cakes

This is a versatile recipe for almost any strong seafood, and the result is increasingly popular. Fish cakes can be prepared in the oven or stove-top, and assembled well in advance of cooking.

2	cups cooked salmon or crab
1	cup grated cheese, cheddar, Swiss
1	cup bread crumbs or equivalent
1	tablespoon grated onion
½	teaspoon salt
½	teaspoon celery salt
	pepper to taste
1	egg, beaten
⅔	cup milk
2	tablespoons melted butter

Flake the salmon or crab and mix well with all other ingredients. Form by hand into desired shape. Loafs are best baked in a 350 degree oven in a buttered pan for 10-15 minutes, whereas smaller cakes can be cooked somewhat faster stove-top in a buttered skillet, allowing ample room between cakes.

Serve with crisp green salad, cabbage salad, or fruit compote. Tartar or remoulade sauce completes the picture.

Carbohydrates: about 7 grams per serving

Suggested wines: Chardonnay, Semillon Blanc, Rose

Favorite family supper

Salmon or crab cakes provide the basis for many supper menus. Here is just one example:

Arrange plates with one cake at center and cover with "simple cheese sauce" (p. 63). Add mustard cabbage wedges (p. 84). Sliced tomatoes, either fresh or canned, may be added to the plate, garnished with sour cream, flavored with herbs such as dill—and you have what is called 'saucedish salad'. Provide drinks and bread, as desired, and this becomes a complete meal, without need for dessert.

Carbohydrates: 28 grams per serving

Creamed tuna with soufflé topping

1   7-oz. can tuna, or fresh equivalent, steamed
1   can condensed cream of mushroom soup
1   handful chopped green pepper (or pimento)
½   cup milk
4   eggs, separated
     dash of baking soda

Combine everything but eggs and soda in a 1½-qt. casserole dish, and place in 375 degree pre-heated oven. Lightly salt egg whites and beat until stiff. Stir some pepper and soda into egg yolks and whisk, then fold into whites. Pour this mixture over the hot tuna and allow to bake until browned—just a few minutes. Crunchy tuna salad, p. 102, can be made easily from this base.

Carbohydrates: about 7 per serving

Steaming clams

Scrub clams with stiff brush under running cold water—discarding any with opened shells. Boil a small amount of water in a large kettle, add clams, cover tightly and return to boil, Watch after a few minutes for shells to open. Remove them as they open and place them in soup dishes for serving—about 10-15 per person.

The hot broth left in the kettle may be strained, then served to guests, with lemon slice, as a small appetizer.

Melted butter is a traditional dip to accompany clams.

Carbohydrates: depending on size, 12-15 per serving

Steamed clam feast

The above ingredients provide everything but a salad and bread to complete a meal, or indeed a feast. Garlic French bread is a natural—use slivered garlic cloves sautéed in butter to coat the bread, and place under broiler for browning. The salad should be well-seasoned to match the clams and broth and bread. The nice part about such a menu is that only the bread need be timed: serve it last.

Carbohydrate: about 30 per feaster

Frozen lobster tails, the easy way

There's nothing like fresh lobster, but the frozen variety comes in handy, especially far from New England. Small or large individually, the frozen tails can be cooked the same way. As this is a rich entrée, you may provide as little as three ounces per serving, as part of an overall menu.

Allow the tails to thaw in their own good time, in the refrigerator—about a day. You'll want to broil them for best results. You may choose to 'butterfly' each tail for appearance sake, by inserting a sharp knife down the center of the underside of the tail, and spreading it by hand. Or you may place the shell-side up under the broiler for a few minutes.

If you choose not to butterfly, use a skewer to hold the underside of the tail from curling up while broiling. On low broil, watch the undersides for excessive browning.

Boiling the tails is also easy. In this case, you need not defrost them. Simply plunge into boiling water, with salt and bay leaf, or cloves. Only a few minutes will be needed for ample cooking. You may then serve with drawn butter, as above. Or you may pull the cooked meat from the shell and use, chilled, in a salad or other dish.

Carbohydrates: none

Skillet shrimp and crabmeat

Shellfish such as crab or shrimp allows for simple preparation stovetop. Simply heat a tablespoon of butter, with onion and garlic as desired, in a skillet, and add cooked or canned shellfish.

Naturally, fresh is best. Choose Dungeness crab in season and shrimp-in-shell for sautéing. Soft-shell crab is a rare treat, also, generally available fresh only in season on the East Coast and Gulf Coast. Deep-frying is an option but is not in the spirit of lower carbohydrate and fat.

A flourish in serving any of the above is to flame a tablespoon of brandy over the cooked shellfish. Lemon, salt and pepper seasoning, a wedge of toast, and voila! a perfect snack.

Carbohydrate: very little

> ### Little shellfish or tuna suppers
>
> 1. Shellfish with apple wedges and cheese: arrange above recipe over Melba toast and serve, on the side, a few slices of sharp cheese and tart, crisp apple. Diet cola, tea or coffee, or a crisp white wine complete the picture.
> 2. Creamed tuna with soufflé topping (p. 24) is complemented nicely with a green bean salad (p. 100) and English muffins, lightly toasted and buttered.
>
> **Carbohydrate: about 20 per serving**
>
> *Wine recommendation: dry sherry or full-bodied Chardonnay*

How to cook Dungeness crab

Most of the West Coast of the United States is blessed with Dungeness crab from about mid-November to March, depending on how far north or south one is. But more than any other shell fish, this one requires care in cooking if purchased live. And live is definitely best, as you will see from the following description.

The way to ruin this delicacy is to boil it indiscriminately, and allow it to continue cooking even after being removed from the pot. There are two rules:

First, Dungeness requires 18 minutes of boiling, after plunging a live crab into a boiling pot, with a tablespoon of rock salt, and returning to boil. Anything less may not be dangerous, as in uncooked fish, but leaves the flesh simply uncooked and lacking in full flavor.

Second, the crab must be chilled immediately after removal from the pot to stop cooking. A large container of cold or iced water will do. If the crab continues to cook, as is the case in much commercial preparation, it becomes mushy. No doubt customers who flock to Fisherman's Wharf in San Francisco still enjoy the crab plucked from the warm pots that greet them everywhere, but they don't taste as good as the real thing.

Large commercial purveyors of cracked crab follow the above rules. Why not you?

Further fish lines

Fillets hold together better than steaks. The latter, though less expensive, also have waste in skin and bones, which require time to remove (after cooking).

Fresh fish has virtually no odor. Consider this in buying.

Skinning fish is always easier after steaming or boiling.

Tomatoes cook well with fish because of their acidity. The Spanish are masters of cooking large fish, such as turbot or halibut, in a bath of sautéed fresh tomatoes.

Many herbs enhance fish during cooking: basil, chervil, dill, marjoram, thyme, parsley, oregano, bay leaf, chives, green onion (scallions), red and green bell pepper. Use them per your preference.

Some firm fish, such as mahi mahi, can be substituted for chicken in various recipes.

Sturgeon has all the flavor strength of beef, and can be served with a mushroom gravy as effectively as a fillet mignon.

Bottom line: there is a range of choices in seafood that we never dreamed of fifty years ago!

3
MEAT DISHES
MEN GO FOR

Meats take the sting out of dieting. They are popular. They present no big carbohydrate problem, so long as they are not overdressed with starchy sauces or trimmings. What's more, a good big serving of beef or chicken or turkey gives such a pleasant feeling of satisfaction it's relatively easy to forgo the usual weight-producing accompaniments.

The recipes for meat and poultry in this chapter range from zero carbohydrate content in rather plain meals to reasonably low amounts in casseroles, stews, and special dishes that make up the main part of the meal. They also run reasonably low in fat. This is good news for anyone of any age or state of health, and is an important factor in the diet of every heart patient or anyone with heart disease.

If you have been ordered or advised to cut down stringently on animal fats, use vegetable oils, such as olive or canola oil, in these recipes. Trim off all visible fat from steaks, chops, pot roasts, or stew meat before cooking. If salt is restricted, avoid corned beef, cured meats such as ham or bacon, and such otherwise good things as pickles, relishes, and appetizers. You will find further discussion of this in Chapter 12, "Special cases, special paces."

About ground meats and other skillet candidates

When you plan to have ground beef, don't buy already-ground hamburger, which has, legally, a fairly high proportion of fat. Instead, ask for lean chuck or bottom round, have the butcher trim off the fat, and ask him to put it through the grinder just once. This way it will remain juicy and not too tightly packed. Handle it lightly.

Use as little oil in the pan as necessary. For sautéing, pan-broiling, or other stove-top cooking, cut down on fat by using a good heavy skillet with Teflon lining.

When you wish to brown steaks, chops, veal cutlets and the like, remember just three simple rules:

1. Wipe each piece of meat dry with a paper towel.
2. Have oil in the skillet very hot before placing meat in pan.
3. Don't overcrowd the pan. You won't need any flouring if you follow these three rules and choose a Teflon pan.

You may safely save, for future use in soups or stews, the fat that accumulates in skillets or roasting pans. Just remember to chill the drippings and remove the hardened fat on top before storing the meat juices.

Even after removing the drippings, the skillet or roasting pan will still be coated with a rich brown glaze, well worth savoring. Don't just wash it in the sink! Deglaze it by adding a small amount of water, broth, wine, or even coffee and stir over heat. Boil down a little and spoon the liquid over the meat.

Savory chopped steaks

Shape a pound or so of freshly ground, lean beef chuck or round into three or four fairly thick patties. Make a deep thumbprint in the top of each; drop about ½ teaspoon butter into each print, then fill with Worcestershire sauce up to a teaspoon, according to your liking.

Heat a heavy skillet, such as cast iron, very hot on the range. At the same time turn on broiler to preheat. Sprinkle skillet lightly with salt, put in patties, and sear for about three minutes. Don't turn them; instead, slide skillet and all under broiler, three or four inches from flame, and broil a few minutes for rare. The hot pan cooks the meat from bottom as the butter and sauce bubble over the surface, resulting in a rich and elegant glaze.

Carbohydrates: less than 1 gram per serving

Hamburger dinner plate

Generous hamburgers, each garnished with three French-fried onion rings (available frozen or in cans)
- Buttered cauliflower (1 cup per serving) dashed with paprika
- Celery and dill pickle strips to take the place of salad
- Dietetic canned fruit cocktail (½ cup per serving) with one tablespoon diced red apple added for color and crunch

Carbohydrates: approximately 24 grams per serving, including an estimated 3 grams for onion rings

Meatza Pies

Cross hamburgers and pizza this way and you have a 'crustless' main dish practically devoid of carbohydrates.

For three generous servings allow a little more than a pound of fresh-ground lean beef, chuck, or bottom round. (As we have seen, ordinary hamburger with its high fat content is avoidable.) Handling as little as possible, shape meat into three individual flat patties, as thick or thin as you prefer.

Heat a heavy skillet sizzling hot. Sprinkle salt lightly in pan, put in the meat, and cook over high heat 3 or 4 minutes, until browned on underside. Turn.

Now add a pizza-style topping as they cook: pinch of oregano, thin tomato slice, Mozzarella, cheddar, or jack cheese next, perhaps some snippets of salami, and finally a sprinkling of grated Parmesan. Slip skillet under broiler for a brief moment to melt and brown cheese. The Meatza pies are ready to go!

Carbohydrates: about 1 gram per serving

Chinese beef with peppers...or Supper in a skillet for two

Get meat and vegetables ready in advance. The actual cooking then goes fast, and you don't need exact measurements.

½   lb. lean beef, cut in strips
1   cup sliced or quartered fresh mushrooms
½   cup coarsely chopped onion
1   cup sliced celery
1   medium green pepper, cut in strips
    Butter and oil
    Garlic salt
    Soy sauce
    Salt and pepper

For the meat, you must use flank steak, round, top sirloin, or filet tails.

About 15 minutes before serving, heat a tablespoon of butter with a teaspoon of oil in a skillet over high heat. Put in the mushrooms and cook for 2 or 3 minutes, then transfer them to a second pan over low heat, to keep warm. Add a little more butter and oil to the first skillet and put in the strips of beef, cooking fast until just rare by turning and stirring for a few minutes. Add the meat to the mushroom pan, and sprinkle with garlic salt.

Now add onion and celery to the first skillet with a few tablespoons of water. Cook quickly 3 or 4 minutes. Add green pepper and cook 2 more minutes. Vegetables should still be crisp. Finally, return the meat and mushrooms from the warming pan to the larger skillet. A touch of soy sauce, salt and pepper and it's ready to serve. Tip: always serve a hot dish on hot plates, warmed in oven or microwave.

Carbohydrates: 11 per serving

Suggested wine: Zinfandel or Syrah

Beef Pot Roast Deluxe

Richly glazed with its own goodness, pot roast done this way is far different from the all-too-usual, drowned-in-water type. It does take some attention during cooking, but no real work.

To serve five or six, with some left over for later use, buy a 3½ to 5 lb. piece of blade-bone or '7-bone' chuck roast, about 3 inches thick. Trim off excess suet; place a piece of it into a Dutch oven or heavy kettle to melt. Wipe meat dry with paper towel after thorough washing. No need to flour it.

When enough fat has melted just to cover bottom of kettle, remove suet, turn to high heat, and put in meat. Brown well on both sides, about 20 minutes total. Peel and slice a garlic clove, add salt, and spread on top of roast. Repeat with small onion. Add no water. Cover and let simmer for 30 minutes. Turn, add a little salt, and simmer for another 30 minutes.

Meat juices and fat will have pooled in the kettle. Remove roast in order to pour off liquid, return to kettle with some liquid. Place juices in shallow container in freezer compartment to solidify and remove fat at top. Return some of the juices to kettle.

Pepper, salt, cover, and simmer for a final 30 minutes. Meanwhile, steam vegetables of your choice.

Take up meat on a hot platter for serving, with vegetables arranged around it. Bones should loosen and can be removed, but keep platter warm in oven.

Now, to make a sauce for the roast or gravy, add ½ cup water to the kettle and heat, stirring, to dissolve all browned bits. This can be spooned over roast just before serving. For gravy, add a cup more water, then add 1 tablespoon cornstarch. Or use 2 tablespoons flour dissolved in warm water. Cook while stirring for a few minutes. Season to taste and serve on the side.

Carbohydrates: 3-4 grams per average serving with sauce, and 15-18 grams overall in thickened gravy. Use gravy sparingly!

Suggested wine: Burgundy or Pinot Noir, or any 'big' red

Boiled Beef with Horseradish

According to men who travel a great deal and like to eat well on the road, old-fashioned boiled beef is one of the most popular items on menus of fine restaurants. Why isn't it served more often at home? Perhaps it takes a while to cook, but it requires little watching or bother.

Use any of the lesser cuts of beef: plate, brisket (not corned), short ribs, bottom round, or rump about 4 or 5 lbs. Wash thoroughly and place in a deep kettle with enough water to cover about half the meat. Heat to boiling and add these (or more) seasonings:

1   **medium onion, peeled and stuck with 2 cloves**
1   **carrot sliced**
2   **outer stalks of celery, with leaves, cut in short lengths**
     Sprigs of parsley, 1 bay leaf, garlic, peppercorns
2   **teaspoons salt**

Cover and let simmer, that is, barely bubble, never boil hard, for 2 to 4 hours. That's right. The meat has to become very tender. The exact time depends on cut of beef and thickness.

Take up meat and strain broth, discarding vegetables and seasonings. Place meat back into hot broth. Taste, and season with salt and fresh-ground black pepper.

If you like, and your carbohydrate count for the day will allow it, you can cook some carrots, green beans, and potatoes separately and add them, hot, to the kettle. Small Dutch onions, available in cans, are also a nice addition. Several serving options: serve the meat sliced, hot or cold with chilled prepared horseradish. Or serve soup-style in shallow bowls with meat and vegetables in the broth. Or include French bread for dipping.

Carbohydrates: negligible for meat, various for vegetables

Wine suggestion: try a crisp Sauvignon Blanc with a cold serving or soup-style; Cabernet Sauvignon goes well with hot, sliced serving and bread.

Corned Beef at its Best

Choose a 4-lb. roast, corned beef bottom round or rump. This is plenty for five or six people, with leftovers for sandwiches or hash. Unfortunately, corned beef is not available much of the time, so focus on the March 17 opportunity!

Cover roast in water in a deep kettle, heat to boiling, skim off foam, and add a variety of seasonings: bay leaf, several whole cloves and peppercorns, peeled cloves of garlic, small chopped onion, celery tops, sliced carrot, and parsley sprigs. Simmer at lowest heat, barely bubbling, for 4-5 hours. The meat will shrink less and become more tender the slower the simmer. You can prepare this well in advance: refrigerate, after cooking, in its own, strained juices. Then serve either hot or cold.

A leg of pork can be done in a similar way, but requires less cooking time, by almost a half.

Carbohydrates: none in either beef or pork, and the rendered broth has only a few.

Wine suggestion: Merlot or Shiraz to match the season

Corned Beef Dinner—Today's Way

- Corned beef, hot or cold, with plain mustard sauce (see p. 60)
- Glazed onions (see p. 89)
- Skillet cabbage (see p. 84)
- Rye bread, half slices
- Cheese-stuffed celery
- Coffee

In kitchen arrange beef, onions and cabbage on hot dinner plates, sprinkling cabbage with paprika for color. Garnish each plate with a celery stalk and perhaps add a few radishes. Serve bread and mustard at the table

Carbohydrates: 26 grams per serving, mainly bread

Wine suggestion: any daily red, with a Riesling or Gewurztraminer with cold corned beef

---

Tenderloin Tips in Brown Mushroom Sauce

Bubbling hot in a big chafing dish, electric skillet, or heated casserole, this is a dramatic dish to serve at a buffet supper for eight or ten guests. For the family, you'll probably make the whole recipe, and freeze half of it for later use.

Make the Brown Mushroom Sauce in advance:

½ lb. sliced fresh mushrooms
4 tablespoons butter
4 tablespoons flour
1 can condensed bouillon (10½ oz.)
½ cup water
½ cup Burgundy wine
   Salt and pepper to taste

Saute mushrooms in butter in a large skillet about five minutes. Sprinkle with flour until flour begins to brown. Immediately add bouillon and water and simmer while stirring until liquid thickens without lumps. Add wine, season to taste, and simmer again. Cool and refrigerate until ready to complete recipe.

When ready to prepare tenderloin tips, about thirty minutes before serving, heat the mushroom sauce in a large skillet, thinning with more wine or water as needed. Then cook over high heat, in butter and oil, in a separate pan, with salt and pepper:

3 lbs. beef tenderloin tips, thinly sliced
2 green peppers, sliced in strips
1 can pimientos, cut in strips (4-oz.)

Allow the tips to brown with plenty of room, and transfer them to the mushroom sauce when still rare. Continue until all tips are cooked, adding more butter and oil as needed. Finally, sauté the green peppers in drippings remaining in the skillet, and add most of them and most of the pimientos to the meat and sauce. Keep the sauce hot but do not boil. Serve in chafing dish, sprinkling remaining pepper/pimiento mixture on top. This elegant dish serves 12 easily, about 2½ quarts in all.

Carbohydrates: about 4 per serving

Suggested wine: Cabernet Sauvignon or Pinot Noir

Swedish Meatballs for Eight

These light, delicate meatballs are unexpectedly low in carbohydrate and can easily be prepared in advance:

½	lb. lean pork, ground
1	lb. beef chuck, ground
1½	teaspoon salt
¼	teaspoon pepper
⅓	teaspoon each nutmeg and allspice
1½	teaspoon cornstarch
½	cup light cream or half-and-half
½	cup water
1	cup fluffy bread crumbs
1	large or 2 small eggs
3	tablespoons finely chopped onion
2	tablespoons butter

For the gravy:

1	can consomme or bouillon (10½ oz.)
1	cup sauterne or dry white wine
1	tablespoon cornstarch

Combine the meat in a large bowl. Mix salt, pepper, other spices, and cornstarch and sprinkle over meat. Heat cream with a little warm water and add bread crumbs. Let cool to lukewarm, then add eggs and beat with a fork. Add to meat. Sauté onions in butter in a large, Teflon skillet, to be used later for browning meatballs. Add to meat and mix thoroughly.

Lay out wax paper on working surface and, with a small spoon, drop on it about 60 small scoops of the meat mixture, in batches as convenient. With moistened hands shape the scoops into balls.

In the skillet used to sauté the onions, brown the meatballs 8 or 10 at a time, in butter, turning them over and over to keep them round. Remove to casserole in batches, adding butter to pan as needed.

For the thin gravy, heat consommé and wine in the skillet containing residual butter/meatball fat. Mix cornstarch with water and add at once to skillet, stirring briskly and cooking just 1-2 minutes, until clear. Season as needed. Pour over meatballs in casserole, cover, and bake at 325 degrees 30-45 minutes. Serve hot. As an entrée, this serves 8 people.

For cocktail party hors d'oeuvres, instead of gravy simply deglaze the skillet with a few spoonfuls of water or wine, stir over heat, and pour over meatballs. Then bake as above.

Carbohydrates: a little more than 5 per serving as an entrée. Gravy or glaze adds less than a gram

Wine suggestion: Merlot, Shiraz, or an oaky Chardonnay

Texas Chili Con Carne

Where they like it hot, they call for this, but you may reduce the chili powder to taste:

4	tablespoons oil
3	cloves minced garlic
2	lbs. ground beef
3	tablespoons chili powder
1½	tablespoons paprika
1	teaspoon cumin seed
3	chili tepines, crushed

Heat oil in a large, heavy kettle. Add garlic, meat, seasonings, with salt and pepper, and cook very slowly about 2 hours, stirring occasionally. Add a few cups of water and continue cooking for another hour. Serve hot in bowls. Serves six.

Carbohydrates: little for anything but seasonings.

Wine suggestion: any hearty red

Paper Plate Smorgasbord

On buffet table arrange these attractive offerings:
- Platter of meat loaf slices on strips of leaf lettuce, with garnish of red onion rings and radishes
- Shallow bowl of anchovy-seasoned deviled eggs in nest of parsley
- Plate holding tall mold of wine-flavored aspic surrounded by crisp lettuce cups, each holding chunks of marinated salmon and cucumber or dill-pickle slices
- Relish dish of ripe olives and small pickled beets
- Baskets of party-size rye bread slices.

Guests should be able to enjoy a serving of everything without exceeding…

Carbohydrates: 21 grams per person

Wine suggestion: Spicy whites, such as Sauvignon Blanc, White Zinfandel, or dry Gewurtztraminer

Special Meat Loaf

An old favorite coming back into popularity, even at restaurants:

1   lb. ground beef or veal
¼   lb. ground lean pork
3   tablespoons finely chopped onions
1   cup soft bread crumbs
1   egg, beaten
½   cup milk

Combine all ingredients, mixing well with salt and pepper to taste. Pack firmly into well-greased loaf pan, and bake in hot oven (400 degrees) for 20 minutes. Then reduce heat to 350 degrees and bake for another 45 minutes. A generous six servings.

Carbohydrates: about 7 per serving, in onions and bread crumbs

Wine suggestion: For this simple recipe, a red of your preference

Pork Chops with Sauerkraut

Perhaps the simplest recipe in this book, and an old time favorite for a winter evening.

1	can (16 oz.) sauerkraut
½	cup white wine
2-4	thick loin pork chops

This is a simple layer idea: the sauerkraut in the bottom of a baking pan, big enough to hold the chops in one layer on top of them. Be sure to rinse the kraut one time or more to reduce acidity, and to trim the chops carefully. Then simply bake in wine at 275 degrees, relatively low temperature, with no more spices than salt and pepper on top the chops, for about three hours, covered tightly. They'll brown by themselves in the last 30 minutes.

The chops will come out with nice rosy tops and a rich flavor if you add additional spice, a tablespoon of catsup and a teaspoon of Worcestershire sauce with the salt and pepper.

You may also substitute fresh celery, onion, and carrot for the sauerkraut, simply slicing them up to cover the bottom of the pan as above.

Carbohydrates: 4 grams per half cup serving. Another 4 if you choose the catsup topping.

Wine suggestion: The biggest Chardonnay you can find, or any other white with plenty of tartness.

Easy-Does-It Dinner

- Baked pork chops with sauerkraut (above)
- Baked winter squash
- Halves of winter pear with cheddar cheese for dessert

Whatever variety of winter squash you choose, servings should not exceed a half cup (12 grams of carbohydrate). The idea is to keep this down to…

Carbohydrates: 29 grams per serving

Fried Ham with Golden Gravy

Select or ask your butcher for a center slice of ham about ½ inch thick. Cut this into three or four serving size pieces. If you've trimmed the fat, use it to brown the ham in a skillet. Next shred a carrot, spread over the ham, and sprinkle with pepper (naturally, without salt). With ham now at low heat, introduce light cream into the pan, just deep enough to almost cover the ham. Don't use milk, which will tend to curdle. Cover and cook gently until carrot seems cooked. The resulting gravy will indeed appear golden, as it is spooned over the ham.

Carbohydrates: 5-7 per serving

Spareribs without Barbecue Sauce

As good as barbecued spareribs are, if the sauce can be avoided there's a special appeal. Here's a simple way to do this, getting rid of most of the fat and bringing out a rich flavor.

Allow a good ½ lb. of pork ribs (not beef, here) per person. If you have a butcher, ask him to crack the ribs through the middle to help the handling of them. Cut the ribs apart, sprinkle with salt and pepper, and, about two hours before serving, place them in a shallow pan in a slow oven (300 degrees) for baking. Fat will pool in the baking pan, so spoon it off three or four times during the two hours. You may also turn the ribs for better heat distribution. They should be browned but not dry after 1¾ hours or so.

Give the ribs an Oriental twist with a mixture of soy sauce, garlic, and hot spices, brushed over them as you turn the ribs.

Carbohydrates: only in the soy sauce, which is relatively sweet

Wine recommendation: whites work well with pork, even with the spices, so try a Pinot Grigio or Viognier

Baked Canadian Bacon

Look for a 2-lb. cut of Canadian bacon at the meat case or your butcher—unsliced. It's not an everyday item. Cook this covered in a deep casserole in about a cup of any wine on hand, spiced with a few cloves or a little cinnamon, if you wish. Two hours at 300 degrees and a little basting will result in a tasty main course, adequate for six or more.

Carbohydrates: less than a gram per serving

Lamb Chops Glazed with Wine

Here's an hour's stove-top cooking project that needs little attention while you prepare the hors d'oeuvres and the rest of the meal. When done they should be richly glazed and fork-tender. For four servings you will need:

4   shoulder lamb chops
1   peeled clove of garlic
3   tablespoons oil
1   medium onion, chopped
¾   cup condensed consommé
½   cup sauterne or other dry white wine

Trim all possible fat from chops and slash edges in several places to keep them from curling. Heat oil and garlic in skillet that has a tight-fitting lid. Brown the chops, salting and peppering them lightly while cooking. The consommé will add some salt. When chops are browned, remove garlic and add onion, consommé and wine. Cover and simmer over low heat until meat is tender and most of the liquid has evaporated. Take up chops on a hot plate and pour off fat from skillet. Deglaze the pan with 2 or 3 tablespoons wine stirred over low heat. Spoon this over the chops and serve.

Carbohydrates: 2 grams per serving

Wine suggestion: Gamay Beaujolais, Gewurztraminer, Zinfandel for plenty of flavor—this applies to most lamb dishes

Broiled Lamb Steaks with Instant Marinade

Purchase rather thin lamb steaks, sometimes called lamb sirloin, about ¾ inch thick. Slash edges to prevent curling. Just before cooking, dip each steak in a mixture of equal parts olive oil, lemon juice, and soy sauce—a scant teaspoon each will be ample for each steak. Broil quickly on charcoal grill or in broiling oven, or even pan-broil in a lightly oiled skillet or stove-top griddle. Sprinkle with salt or garlic salt while cooking. Test by cutting next to the bone. It should be delicately pink for best flavor. Serve at once on warm plates.

Carbohydrates: about 2 grams of the marinade in each serving

Baked Lamb Chops

This is a host's delight: a dish that needn't be closely watched. The sour cream is always a crowd-pleaser:

1   peeled clove of garlic
2   tablespoons oil
4   shoulder lamb chops, trimmed of fat
½   cup sour cream
1   tablespoon vinegar
1   tablespoon Worcestershire sauce
    Paprika or other herbs

Heat garlic in oil in large skillet and brown chops at moderate heat in this flavorsome oil. Remove chops to a shallow baking dish, pour off fat from skillet, and stir the rest of the ingredients into the glazed skillet. Add a little warm water to the mix if it thickens, and season with salt, pepper, and herbs of your choice, such as paprika, thyme, or scallions. Pour this mixture over the chops and place the baking dish with the mixture and chops, uncovered, into a moderate oven. At 350 degrees the chops will be tender in about forty minutes. Serves four.

Carbohydrates: less than 2 grams per serving

Wine suggestion: Cabernet or Merlot

Lamb Shanks Superb

Allow one meaty lamb shank per person. Prepare well in advance by inserting slivers of garlic near the bone and marinating for several hours in soy sauce or red wine. Note that proper cooking will take at least two hours either stovetop or in the oven, in moderate heat, covered. Browning should be done with oregano, marjoram, or thyme, and cooking with chopped onion in a medium red wine. As in most meat dishes, a rich finishing sauce should be prepared by pouring off the fat in the kettle and heating the glaze with a little wine.

Carbohydrates: about 2 per serving

Lamb Shish Kebabs

For a large group of ten or twelve people, a full leg of lamb of 4 lbs. or more will suffice. This recipe is for half that number, and the lamb can be boneless shoulder or other cuts.

2 lbs. boned lamb cut in 1¼ inch cubes
1-2 large onions, chopped
1-2 cloves garlic, crushed with salt
Soy sauce, tarragon wine vinegar, and oil in equal amounts with salt and pepper for small marinade

String the lamb cubes on skewers and place them in a pan that can take the marinade, which is all the rest of the ingredients. Let stand for at least 30 minutes, turning occasionally, and then barbecue or broil in oven until done as preferred.

Option: add equal amount of ham cubes to the skewers, decreasing the cubes of lamb, and alternating on skewers.

Further option: add red or green peppers and mushrooms to the skewers, remembering that these cook much faster than meat and should be on separate skewers, or added after the meat has previously been seared.

Carbohydrates: virtually none, as onion is only in marinade

Wine suggestion: Zinfandel, Pinot Noir, Cabernet Sauvignon

Easy on the Chef

- Baked lamb chops (p. 42)
- Baked shredded carrots
- Chilled, cooked asparagus spears (6) on greens with French dressing
- Canned peach halves (dietetic pack) dotted with whipped cream cheese and dash of cinnamon
- Hot tea or coffee

Note: to prepare shredded raw carrot, 1 cup per serving, bake in a covered, buttered casserole at 350 degrees for 25 minutes.

Carbohydrates: about 25 grams per serving, of which the peach half is about 5 grams

20-minute Herb Marinade for Lamb

You've noticed several of the lamb recipes call for marinating the lamb well in advance of preparation. This is because lamb tends to be rich in flavor and requires balance.

Marinades provide flavor, not tenderness, and long marinating in the refrigerator overnight or even for a day or two shows off the flavor well. Even if all the time you have is twenty minutes, this basic recipe will work well:

> **Crumbled mixed herbs, such as rosemary, thyme, oregano, and basil**
> **Juice of 1 or 2 cloves of garlic**
> **Soy sauce, Worcestershire sauce, and olive oil in equal measure**
> **Vinegar or lemon juice as needed for tartness**
> **Salt, pepper, onion salt to taste, freshly ground as available**
> **Scallions, red onions, peppers, jalapenos as desired and in moderation**

Make enough to cover the meat. There are no carbohydrates in any marinade that 'transfer' to the main dish.

Baked Smoked Tongue

This isn't a popular dish, but one worth exploring. Start with smoked beef tongue purchased as early in the day as possible. It will take 2-3 hours of slow cooking in a kettle, covered with water, and spiced with a sliced onion and some garlic. When tender, the skin and excess fat can be removed. An hour or so before dinner, bake at 350 degrees in a casserole with a mixture of celery and carrots, sliced diagonally, and 2-3 tomatoes sliced to cover top of meat—lightly oiled but with no liquid. The vegetable group can be served alongside the sliced tongue. Serves six.

Carbohydrates: 4 grams per serving, in the vegetables

One-Minute Gravy for Minute Steaks

When you have browned a couple of thin steaks, or lamb or veal chops, or a juicy hamburger in oil in a skillet, don't just remove the meat and wash the pan. Pour off the fat, put the skillet back on heat with a little water or wine. Stir. Now you have a glaze. Add a good spoonful of sour cream, with celery salt and Worcestershire sauce, and you have gravy. One minute!

Baked Veal Chops

Have your butcher chop off excess bone from chops (allow 1-2 per person). Wash and wipe dry with paper towel, sprinkle with salt and pepper. Brown lightly on both sides in heavy skillet in a minimum of butter and oil. Remember: butter browns, oil doesn't. To prepare for oven, top each chop with a tablespoon of sour cream dashed with Worcestershire sauce, then sprinkle with celery salt. Finish with an onion slice topped with Cheddar or Parmesan grated cheese. Cover the heavy skillet and bake at 350 degrees for at least 30 minutes, or until tender. Just before serving, remove cover and allow cheese to brown.

Carbohydrates: About 3 grams per serving, all in the topping

Veal Scallopini Sauterne

The old standard, a very simple way:

  1 **lb. veal round, sliced ¼ inch thick**
  1 **tablespoon butter**
  2 **teaspoons oil**
  1 **clove garlic, crushed**
  ½ **cup Sauterne or other dry white wine**
  ½ **cup hot water**

Cut veal into small pieces, wash, dry with paper towel, sprinkle with salt and pepper. Brown in butter and oil with garlic. Remove garlic and add water and wine; cover and simmer for about 30 minutes.

Add your favorite herbs, such as thyme or marjoram, during cooking. Serves four.

Carbohydrates: None

Suggested wine: Sauvignon Blanc, Viognier, Sauterne, but always check the rest of the meal. An accompaniment like gnocchi might suggest a heartier wine.

Italian Dinner with Innovations

- Antipasto salads
- Saltimbocca, as on next page
- Buttered sliced zucchini, ¾ cup
- Vienna bread
- choice of wine

For antipasto salads, to serve six, in advance prepare garlic olives by marinating pitted black olives in a garlic-olive oil dressing; then drain an 8-oz. can of baby limas and marinate in the same way. Also prepare in advance a few boiled eggs, shelled, and quartered. You may also add salami, shellfish, such as crab legs or prawns, or marinated mushrooms or artichoke hearts. The idea is to offer a range of small nibbles, served on lettuce leaves, on a large salad platter. Garnish with strips of pimiento and a bowl of dipping sauce. The salads are the first course and do not accompany the dinner.

Carbohydrates: about 28 grams per serving, from salads to bread

Wine suggestions: Barolo, Chianti, or California reds

Saltimbocca (Veal and Ham Roll)

These neat little packages take a bit of time to wrap, but they are so good they are worth almost any effort. For six servings you'll want 12 thin pieces of veal, round or rump, about 4 inches square, roughly. Next, an equal number of paper-thin slices of prosciutto, which is Italian ham. Prosciutto is spicy and salty, but otherwise similar to any good baked ham. So you can substitute a good Virginia ham, for example, but make sure the slices are thin.

1½	lbs. thinly sliced veal round or rump
	Chopped parsley
¼	lb. prosciutto
12	small sage leaves, or ½ teaspoon powdered sage
12	thin slices Monterey Jack or Swiss cheese, about ¼ lb.
2	tablespoons olive oil
1	tablespoon butter
¼	cup dry white wine

Pound veal slices with edge of heavy plate until they are very thin. Cut into 4-5 inch rectangles or squares. Sprinkle with salt, pepper and chopped parsley. Place a slice of prosciutto on each piece of veal and trim to fit. Put a sage leaf or a tiny bit of powdered sage on the ham, and then lay a thin slice of cheese over that. Roll up neatly and fasten with toothpicks.

Brown the rolls gently on all sides in hot oil and butter in a skillet. Then add the wine, cover, and let cook very slowly half an hour or longer, until veal is tender and most of the wine has evaporated. You can always add a little more wine and turn the heat lower if the liquid evaporates before the meat appears to be done. Six servings.

Carbohydrates: 4 grams, or less than 1 gram per serving.

Wine suggestion: Burgundy, Pinot Noir, Merlot

Perfect Veal Stew

Perfection here is in the ingredients and method of preparation, both of which are useful in any basic stew. So learn from this:

2	lbs. veal, cubed for stew
	Garlic salt, oil, butter
2	teaspoons chicken stock, or 2 or 3 bouillon cubes, or 2 teaspoons miso soup mix
1	medium onion, chopped
8	whole peppercorns
	Sprigs, celery tops or parsley
2-3	large stalks celery, sliced thinly
2	medium carrots, sliced
12	small canned onions, drained
1	green or red pepper, cut in strips
8	medium mushrooms, sliced

Dry the veal cubes with paper towel. Don't flour them, just spread on waxed paper and sprinkle garlic salt lightly on them. Heat about 1 tablespoon oil and butter in a skillet, Teflon coated if possible, and begin sautéing meat gradually and with ample space. Transfer as they brown on all sides to a heavy kettle, over low heat, as you continue browning of the rest. Add oil and butter as necessary to the browning pan. Save fats in the skillet for use below.

Dissolve chicken stock or bouillon and add to the meat in the kettle, along with onions and peppercorns. Add sprigs, cover, and simmer for 45 minutes or more, until on testing a cube or two meat seems tender. Remove sprigs, add celery and carrots, with hot water if needed. Cover again and cook up to 30 minutes. Meanwhile, sauté the diced mushrooms, pepper, and onions in drippings left in the skillet, and add to the kettle.

You can use cornstarch (½ tablespoon in ¼ cup of water) to thicken the stew, if needed. When seasoned to taste, the stew is ready to serve in hot soup plates, with garlic French bread.

Carbohydrates: about seven per serving

No-Trouble Veal Casserole

Here's a recipe that needs no meat browning: just add the ingredients together and bake! A long bake...

3	lbs. veal, cut for stew
1	medium onion, chopped
½	cup slivered almonds
½	teaspoon rosemary
½	teaspoon marjoram
1	can Cream of Chicken soup

Put meat in a large, shallow casserole and sprinkle with onions, almonds, and herbs. Spread undiluted soup over the top. Cover and bake 1 hour at 300 degrees, then reduce temperature to 250 and continue baking for another two hours. Check occasionally during the last hour to make sure there is enough liquid. Add water as needed. If too liquid, remove cover. Heat can be turned down as needed to fit dinner time. About eight servings

Carbohydrates: about 5 per serving

Oven Fried Chicken with White Wine

This isn't 'Kentucky Fried' but it's basic and good. Choose chicken pieces you and your guests prefer, especially split breasts, thighs, and wings. (Gone are the days when necks, backs, and gizzards were the preferred parts. But many still like to gnaw on bones.) For four people:

1	large chicken, cut into pieces, skin removed
3	tablespoons olive oil and butter, combined
½	cup dry white wine or dry Vermouth
½	teaspoon rosemary
½	teaspoon marjoram

Heat all ingredients together, except chicken, in shallow pan, add chicken pieces, and continue cooking while sprinkling with salt, pepper, and a little paprika. Place in oven at 350 degrees for 30 minutes. Turn over and cook at lower heat for another 30. If guests aren't ready when the chicken is, uncover chicken, put a piece of aluminum foil on top loosely, and simmer on low heat.

Carbohydrates: None

Dinner for Three Couples

- Crab cocktails with wheat crackers
- Oven-fried chicken with white wine (previous page)
- Well seasoned bean sprouts
- Artichokes with melted butter
- Celery and olives
- White wine
- Dessert with apricot brandy

Plan on ½ cup cooked or canned sprouts per serving. Heat in a small amount of chicken broth, sprinkle with seasoned salt of your choice. See p. 78 for artichoke preparation.

Carbohydrates: 24 grams per serving, depending on dessert

Wine suggestion: A tart white, such as Chardonnay, Pinot Grigio, or Viognier

Chinese Chicken and Walnuts

This recipe succeeds or fails on the quality of the chicken. The array of options is overwhelming: 'natural', 'free-range', 'organic', or a combination of the above. Cooking technique has little effect on tenderness. But a recipe like this helps:

1	lb. chicken pieces, boned and skinned
1	onion, sliced
1	green onion, cut in strips
6	mushrooms, sliced
1	cup sliced celery
2	tablespoons cornstarch
2	cups chicken broth
1	cup Chablis or other white table wine
2-3	tablespoons soy sauce
3	tablespoons butter
1	cup toasted California walnut halves (see p. 51)

Saute onion and green pepper in butter for three minutes in a large skillet that can handle all the chicken. Add chicken and cook for another 10 minutes. Add celery. Mix cornstarch with ¼ cup of the cold broth. Add rest of broth, wine, and mushrooms to the chicken mixture. When this is hot, stir in cornstarch and broth and cook, gently, until sauce is bubbling hot and looks clear. Add black pepper and soy sauce to taste. Stir in the toasted walnuts. Good for six servings.

Carbohydrates: 9 grams per serving

Wine suggestion: a light white wine, such as Riesling or Sauvignon Blanc

The walnut halves in the above recipe need some advance planning. You'll want to brown them in a shallow pan in the oven, but first you must boil them in water for 3 minutes and drain well. While the walnuts are cooking, you can brush them with melted butter and sprinkle them with seasoned salt. They can be stored in the refrigerator without loss of flavor.

Baked Chicken Pieces with Lemon and Herbs

If you like chicken breasts, without skin, this is a simple way to get a spicy flavor. Six servings are easily accommodated with six boneless, skinless breasts that are so readily available these days. (Of course you can also use this recipe with other chicken parts you may prefer.) For these you will need:

2	tablespoons melted butter
2	tablespoons lemon juice
½	teaspoon tarragon leaves
½	teaspoon basil leaves, coarsely crumbled
¼	teaspoon thyme

Sprinkle chicken surfaces with salt and pepper as you desire. Line a shallow pan with aluminum foil, oil lightly, and arrange chicken pieces in a single layer. Brush with herb mixture, and bake at 350 degrees for about 40 minutes without turning. Check to see if tender but not overdone. (With bone-in pieces, you can check by seeing if the bones release easily from the meat.)

Brown under the broiler for a few minutes for a nice finish. Basting also helps add the right touch to the chicken.

Carbohydrates: 2 grams overall, mainly from,,, the lemon juice!

Wine suggestion: stay on the tart side with Sauvignon Blanc or Pinot Grigio.

Delicate Stewed Chicken

A whole chicken can yield six to eight individual pieces, if cut properly from a whole chicken. You can do this yourself, or buy individual breasts, thighs, legs, and wings in separate packages. Either will work fine. Wash all pieces thoroughly and marinate, if you have time, in soy sauce, lemon, white wine, or all three, with scallions and peppers as you may have on hand.

3	lbs. chicken, in parts
3	cups water, salted
1	carrot, sliced
1	onion, sliced
2-3	celery tops, with leaves
2-3	parsley sprigs
1	teaspoon chicken stock base, or 2 bouillon cubes
6	peppercorns

Heat all ingredients except chicken in a large pot, and when they come to a boil drop in chicken pieces one by one so as not to stop the boil. Cover and simmer gently 20 minutes or so until chicken appears tender but not overcooked. Take up the pieces and place in a warming pan.

Strain the broth. If too much fat rises to the surface, spoon it off, or chill the broth quickly in the freezer and lift it off.

Presentation:
You can serve the cooked pieces simply by reheating them in the broth and placing them, drained on a platter with chopped parsley on top. Or you can serve in a rich gravy:

Thicken the broth with a tablespoon of cornstarch mixed in cold water, then cooking it while stirring for 2 minutes. You may even add sour cream to thicken the gravy, as in the veal recipes above. Then reheat the chicken pieces in the gravy, and serve.

Carbohydrates: None except for the gravy, about 7 grams per tablespoon

Wine suggestion: Chicken is now so readily available in so many dishes that any decent wine is acceptable with it. With the simple recipe above a Chardonnay is ideal.

Oriental Oven-Fried Chicken

This is a simple method, with some subtleties from the above. Start, again, with the best chicken you can find. We're going to bake this in the oven, in a shallow pan with foil on top. It will take about an hour at 350 degrees. So select as many pieces as you need, either for a dinner party or a lunch, and save the rest for later.

¼   **cup soy sauce**
¼   **cup olive oil**
¼   **cup garlic salt**
1   **teaspoon pepper or other seasonings**

Simply dip the chicken pieces in this mixture (you've seen it before!), arrange the chicken in the pan, and bake. Use the dip another day. Turn the chicken occasionally, during the hour at 350 degrees. Only the soy sauce has any carbohydrates.

Brandy-Creamed Chicken

Disjoint a good-sized fryer-roaster chicken, salt and pepper the pieces, but don't flour. In a big skillet that has a tight-fitting lid heat about two tablespoons butter and oil. Cover the bottom of the skillet with a thin layer of diced onions, put in the chicken, and let cook very gently, turning often until well browned.

Now pour about ½ cup brandy over all. Cover and let simmer slowly, turning occasionally, until tender.

To serve, pour ½ cup heavy cream over all, heat a few minutes, and spoon the resulting gravy over the chicken. You may also add a curry note by adding curry powder to the browned chicken before adding the brandy.

Carbohydrates: 10 grams in the onions and cream.

Wine suggestion: Brandy! But remember where brandy came from: good red wine. So choose your favorite.

Sauteed Chicken Breasts, Bercy

Here is a stove-top version of the above, which results in faster cooking and a more generous sauce.

- **4** boneless, skinless chicken breasts
- **4** tablespoons butter
- **2** tablespoons olive oil
- **2-3** tablespoons chopped shallots or green onions
- **8** sliced mushrooms
- **2** teaspoons minced parsley
- **1** cup dry white wine

About half an hour before serving time (not long!), sprinkle the chicken with salt and pepper and cook quickly in moderately hot butter/oil pan, turning once. Set aside in a warm oven under foil while the sauce is prepared.

Add shallots to the hot drippings in the skillet, cook briefly then add mushrooms and cook for a few more minutes, until browned. Add wine and additional butter to finish the sauce, and ladle over the chicken when ready to serve. Dress with parsley.

Carbohydrates: less than 2 grams per serving

Wine suggestion: Chardonnay

Broiled Chicken with Wine and Herbs

To serve four, have two broiling chickens split, removing the necks and giblets. Simmer these with a sliced onion and bay leaves, in a covered pan for later use. Also add rosemary and marjoram to the broth, and a cup of white table wine to create a basting sauce. Chop giblets fine after cooking, and set aside for another use.

Rub the chicken all over with a combination of garlic, lemon juice, oil or melted butter. Salt and pepper the chicken and place, skin-side down, in a foil-lined shallow pan (not a rack). Place as low as possible under (away from) the broiler, and baste frequently with the herb-wine mixture. Browning will take about 30 minutes. Remove the chicken to a platter in the oven to keep warm.

Thicken the sauce by adding a little flour to the butter and gradually introducing it to the pan. Serve chicken skin-side up with sauce spooned over it.

Carbohydrates: None except for the flour in the sauce

Wine suggestion: Chardonnay or Gewurtztraminer

Chicken Paprika

Saute unfloured chicken pieces, enough for six servings, in a small amount of hot butter-oil mix until browned and tender, seasoning lightly with salt, pepper and paprika during cooking. Save skillet. Transfer chicken to a casserole, cover, and place in a 300 degree oven while you prepare the paprika sauce:

- 2 **tablespoons butter**
- 2 **medium onions, thinly sliced**
- 1 **tablespoon flour**
- 1 **tablespoon paprika**
- 1 **cup sour cream**
- ½ **cup broth, from bouillon cube**

Add a little butter to drippings left in pan and sauté sliced onions, about 5 minutes. Stir in flour and seasonings, salt to taste, and cook 2 minutes. With heat as low as possible, add broth and sour cream, stirring and cooking gently until slightly thickened. Never let the heat reach the point at which the cream separates. Pour over chicken when ready to serve.

Carbohydrates: 5-6 grams per serving, in the sauce

Wine suggestion: any modest white, such as Riesling or Rose

Turkey Roasting Tips

To cut down preptime and lower carbohydrates, roast your turkey unstuffed!
A mere half cup of stuffing adds up to 28 grams of carbohydrates, whereas the
turkey itself has none.

How to prepare: With a frozen turkey, thaw well in advance (do this slowly, in
the refrigerator, allowing 1-3 days depending on size of turkey). Rub cavities
in turkey thoroughly with salt. Skewer wings close to body. Likewise close skin
over neck but leave main cavity open.

Set turkey on its back in a large, shallow pan. Rub skin all over with olive
oil or a little melted turkey fat. Place an apple or large onion in cavity, uncut, to
retain shape.

Roasting: The general rule is to allow about 20 minutes per pound. This means
you take the weight of the bird and divide by three, and the result is roasting
time in hours. Slow cooking is best, at about 325 degrees.

The fresh versus frozen debate goes back and forth. With great improve-
ments in methods of freezing in recent years, some taste panels have come down
for frozen! In any event, do not prepare stuffing in advance (if you prefer to
have it for your guests), and leave in the turkey overnight. There's too much
chance of bacterial growth, and roasting won't correct it!

Cover the bird loosely with aluminum foil, and use a throw-away aluminum roasting pan to avoid cleanup work. Remove the foil for the last half hour
for thorough browning, and baste occasionally during cooking. You can also
dispense with the foil and simply cover the bird with an oiled piece of cheesecloth after it begins to brown.

Important: allow the bird to rest outside the oven for an hour before
serving. Cover the turkey with two or three towels. You will want to draw off
liquids, as you baste, to make gravy. Don't wait until the bird is out of the oven.
If you don't chop up the gizzard and liver to sauté in the gravy mix, you are
wasting the best part of a turkey dinner. You can never have enough gravy!
Hint: cheat a little with a packaged mix.

Holiday Dinner on your Diet

- Oyster cocktail with 2 small crackers
- Turkey roasted without stuffing (or with stuffing for your guests only
- Green and yellow wax beans, canned or frozen, with mushroom added

- Orange and avocado salad with French dressing, arranged on Romaine with a dusting of Parmesan cheese
- White wine or dietetic cranberry juice
- After-dinner mints

Carbohydrates: 32 per serving, including vegetables and dessert

How to make a turkey broth:
While the turkey is roasting, cook the neck, heart, and gizzard in 6-8 cups water. Add a handful of celery tops, a sliced onion, some parsley, and a few peppercorns. Cover and simmer at least an hour, add salt to taste and add liver to cook for 15 minutes more. Then remove and cool giblets, chop up meat for gravy, strain and set aside broth.

How to tell when turkey is done:
A meat thermometer inserted into the thigh should read 185 degrees when done. Also, the drumstick will move freely.

Lift the turkey on to a generous platter, cover with towels as described above, and let rest before bringing to table for carving.

To make giblet gravy

Follow this old-fashioned method that keeps both fat and carbohydrates low.

Take all the drippings you have saved while basting and what remains in the pan, and chill quickly in freezer. After 10-15 minutes, you will be able to remove fat from top. Discard fat. Add the remainder to the broth, as prepared above. For more volume, add canned chicken broth.

Mix 2 tablespoons flour with a little more warm water in a bowl, stirring in the water slowly to avoid lumping. To this thin paste gradually add some of the broth mix, then transfer all to the roasting pan and cook slowly until thickened smoothly. Add chopped giblets. Keep on low heat to cook down to the consistency you prefer. Season with salt and pepper as needed.

Carbohydrates: about 8 grams per cup, or only 2 per normal serving. But watch the potatoes!

4
SAUCES
THAT STEAL THE MEAL

D on't skimp on sauces: you can never have too much.

Most of the sauces given here can be used interchangeably with meat, fish, eggs, and vegetables. Don't be hesitant about trying combinations other than those suggested, nor about omitting and adding seasonings to suit your personal preferences. Check the tables at the back of the book, of course, if you have any doubt about the carbohydrate count.

Speaking of seasonings, it's wise for weight watchers to keep a good variety on hand, and get into the habit of trying new ones. Possibilities are endless: fresh, frozen, or freeze-dried chives, green and red peppers, parsley. The onion family: shallots, scallions or green onions, garlic, leeks. All sorts of seasoned salt. And of course the dried herbs and spices in several arrays of racks in the supermarket.

In addition to the recipes in this chapter, check the "sauces" listing in the index for others elsewhere in the book.

Special Sauce for Broiled Lobster

Slightly less rich than the usual clarified butter, this flavorful sauce is well worth serving with broiled fresh lobster halves or frozen lobster tails.

While the broiling is proceeding, melt 2 tablespoons butter in a small frying pan for two servings. Add 2-3 tablespoons of light cream, with a dash of Worcestershire sauce. When the lobsters are done, add whatever drippings are left in the broiling pan, heat, stirring, and serve in a sauce boat or small heated pitcher. You and your guest can pour the sauce over the lobster in the shell. It is best to keep the boats or small cups heated to prevent the sauce from congealing.

Seafood Cocktail Sauce

Here's the all-time favorite. The anchovy paste makes the difference.

- 1   cup mayonnaise
- 2   tablespoons catsup
- 1   tablespoon tarragon wine vinegar
- 1   tablespoon anchovy paste
      Tabasco sauce and pepper to taste

Simply mix all ingredients and chill. Ideal for shrimp or crabmeat, enough for five servings.

Carbohydrates: about 3 grams per ¼ cup serving

Almondine Sauce

This quick sauce is served hot, usually on fried or boiled trout, filet of sole, halibut, or cod. It is equally good on green beans, broccoli, asparagus, snap peas, or even spinach.

Heat 4 tablespoons butter in a skillet and gradually add ¼ cup shaved or slivered almonds. Heat until nuts are brown. Sprinkle lightly with salt; add 2 tablespoons lemon juice, let foam up for a minute, and serve in warmed boat. Makes 3-4 servings.

Carbohydrates: about 3 grams per serving

Olive-Almond Sauce for Broiled Fish

Another almond sauce, but what a difference the onions and olives make!

- 1 cup sour cream
- ¼ cup mayonnaise
- ¼ cup pimiento-stuffed olives, chopped
- 2 tablespoons grated onion, or 1 green onion finely chopped
- 2 tablespoons coarsely chopped salted almonds
- 2 tablespoons lemon juice

Combine ingredients, salt and pepper to taste. Chill. Makes about 1½ cups, enough for a dozen servings.

Carbohydrates: about 1½ grams per full tablespoon

Fluffy Cucumber Sauce

This is a favorite for poached salmon, cold or warm. The dill is the key:

- ½ medium cucumber
- ½ cup whipping cream
- ¼ cup mayonnaise
- ½ teaspoon dill weed
- 1 tablespoon vinegar
  Dash of cayenne pepper

Pare the cucumber, chop fine or shred on medium-coarse grater. Squeeze out excess juice with doubled cheese cloth. Whip the cream and fold in mayonnaise and cucumber. Season to taste with salt and freshly ground black pepper. Chill. Versatile enough for cold cuts or any steamed fish.

Carbohydrates: about 2 grams per serving, of 5-6 servings

Plain Hot Mustard

The standard is Coleman's (English) dry mustard, but it's also available in bulk. Simply stir in cold water or white wine and let stand for 20 minutes (important). Serve with mayonnaise and lemon as a cracked crab sauce, or use wherever a good hot mustard is needed, such as a cold-cut sandwich.

Louis Dressing for Crab or Shrimp

This classic dressing for Crab Louis answers the question, "What dressing do you want on your crab salad?"

1	cup mayonnaise
¼	cup French dressing
¼	cup chili sauce
1	small onion, grated
2	tablespoons chopped stuffed olives
1	tablespoon chopped parsley
1	tablespoon tarragon wine vinegar
1	tablespoon prepared horseradish
1	teaspoon Worcestershire sauce

Combine ingredients. Chill. Garnish salad with halves of hardboiled egg or tomato wedges. Use also as a cocktail sauce for shrimp. This recipe is enough for 4-6 salads, or 6-7 cocktail-style servings, but you might want to double it for later.

Carbohydrates: about 2 grams per rounded tablespoon

Sauce Verte

Take the mystery out of this French-type sauce: the green color is added simply with herbs:

1	cup mayonnaise
2	tablespoons chopped chives or scallion tops
1	tablespoon chopped parsley
1½	tablespoons tarragon-flavored white wine vinegar

Combine ingredients and salt and pepper to taste. You may add green food color for effect. Chill. Good, and good-looking, on hot or cold poached salmon.

Carbohydrates: just 1 gram per rounded tablespoon

Remoulade Sauce

Another French classic, but so easy to make you will never again be intimidated by the name!

1   cup mayonnaise
¼   cup finely chopped dill pickle
1   tablespoon drained capers
1   teaspoon prepared mustard, or dry mustard
1   tablespoon chopped parsley
½   teaspoon dry chervil or tarragon leaves, crumbled

Mix ingredients and taste. Add a little onion, garlic salt, or even white pepper, as you prefer. Chill. Excellent for hot or cold vegetables or fish fillets. Enough for 6-8 servings.

Carbohydrates: 3 grams per serving

Tartar Sauce

This is the universal sauce at seafood counters, fast food emporiums, and even fine restaurants. Many of the latter claim their own special ingredients (even mashed potatoes!). Here are the basics:

½   cup mayonnaise
1   tablespoon chopped dill pickle
1   tablespoon chopped green olives or capers
1-2 tablespoons minced chives
1   tablespoon minced parsley
    Lemon juice, Tabasco sauce to taste

Combine ingredients. Chill. Serve with any fish, especially broiled or fried sole, rex sole, Petrale, halibut, cod, white fish.

You'll want to make a batch sufficient for several dishes, if you like fish. There's little in this basic recipe that conflicts with any wine choice, naturally, white.

Carbohydrates: only a gram per serving in this home-made recipe

Genuine Sauce Mornay

Here the heroes are cheese, Parmesan and Swiss, so notice the lack of the usual herbs:

- 2 tablespoons butter
- 2 tablespoons flour
- 1 cup chicken broth
- ½ cup milk
- ¼ cup grated Parmesan cheese
- ¼ cup grated Swiss cheese
- ½ cup light or heavy cream

Melt butter over low heat. Make a paste of a little of the broth added gradually to the flour; adding it directly to butter will tend to lump. Stir until flour, broth, and butter are smooth, then add milk and simmer 5 minutes, to cook the flour. Add grated cheese and seasonings, such as salt and pepper to taste. Finally, stir in cream and serve. Makes about 2½ cups, excellent for asparagus, broccoli, and fish roll-ups.

Carbohydrates: about 3 grams per ¼ cup, or one serving, of sauce

Simple Cheese Sauce

The small difference here is the emphasis on spiciness from the mustard, instead of the chicken broth, as above.

- 2 tablespoons butter
- 2 tablespoons flour
- ¼ teaspoon dry mustard, such as Coleman's
  Dash of white pepper
- 1 cup milk
- 1 cup, or ¼ lb., grated Cheddar cheese

Here again take care to avoid lumps by adding a little liquid—here, milk—to the flour gradually as it's mixed, and only then stirring into melted butter. When the roux is smooth, add mustard and cheese gradually at low heat. Stir all the way.

Feel free to experiment with other seasonings than salt and pepper. Keep the consistency a little on the thin side: it will tend to thicken as it cools.

The result is a perfectly usable sauce for vegetables and fish of many kinds, about 1½ cups or enough for six people.

Carbohydrates: about 4 grams per serving, mainly the flour

Sauce Lamaze

Don't let this list of ingredients scare you. They're commonly available but also can be omitted here and there without great effect. The pickle relish and the egg are the highlights.

- 1 **cup mayonnaise**
- ⅓ **cup chili sauce**
- ¼ **cup drained sweet pickle relish**
- 1 **hard-boiled egg, finely chopped**
- 2 **tablespoons finely chopped celery**
- 1 **teaspoon finely chopped pimiento**
- 1 **teaspoon finely chopped green pepper**
- 1 **teaspoon chopped chives**
- 1 **prepared mustard, or dry mustard**
- 1 **teaspoon Worcestershire sauce**
  Paprika, dash

Mix ingredients and chill. Makes about 2 cups. Ideal to keep on hand for the occasional fish or vegetable dish that would seem boring in tartar sauce or melted butter.

Carbohydrates: less than 2 grams per rounded tablespoon, a normal serving

Homemade Mayonnaise

You've noticed how many of the sauce recipes here begin with mayonnaise. There's nothing wrong with the leading brands. But homemade has great appeal. Why not try it, the way your grandmother made it, and the great chefs still do.

We're talking olive oil, egg yolks, lemon (or vinegar), and salt and pepper. It's a small chemistry experiment: how to create a mix that brings oil and water together: an emulsion. The secret is in which ingredient to start with and how to add the other.

Start with the egg yolk, stirred with salt and pepper, and maybe even a little garlic. Very slowly, drop by drop, add olive oil. Stir, or, better, whisk briskly. At some point, after a dozen drops of oil, the mix will "take," or become firm. Now you can continue to add oil more generously. When you've reached the proportion you want, much more oil than egg yolk, "fix" the process by adding lemon or vinegar, always stirring. With the real egg, exceptional olive oil, and that touch of garlic, there's no bottled mayonnaise that can touch it.

5
DAIRY DELIGHTS

The best supplements to meat and fish are eggs and cheese. An egg or an ounce of cheese is equal in protein to an ounce of cooked, lean meat.

But that's not the whole story. The semi-hard varieties of cheese are concentrated sources of the calcium in milk. An ounce, or a 1-inch cube of cheese, equals ⅔ cups milk. Both cheese and egg yolks are rich in phosphorous, so important along with calcium for good teeth and bones. And egg yolks are also a rich source of iron.

When you add to these nutritional benefits the facts that eggs and cheese are also inexpensive and readily available, you can see why they are so popular. As it happens, they are also low in carbohydrates, yet high enough in fat content to give the feeling of satiety. This is why eggs and cheese are indispensable in the Drinking Man's Diet.

So let's explore the simple egg recipes and see how they can work toward a full diet plan.

All egg recipes you come across in your reading are merely outgrowths of the standard ways of cooking eggs. These Chive-Cheese Scrambled Eggs, for example, are simply scrambled eggs with cream cheese, with water in place of milk, plus seasonings. For plain scrambled eggs, a good rule is 1 tablespoon of milk to each egg, but it's always your choice for how you like your eggs.

Chive-Cheese Scrambled Eggs

- 6 **eggs**
- 2 **tablespoons water**
- ½ **teaspoon seasoned salt**
  Dash of pepper
- 2 **tablespoon butter**
- 1 **3-oz. package cream cheese, crumbled**
- 1 **tablespoon freeze dried or fresh chopped chives (substitute, also, scallion tops)**

Add water, seasoned salt and pepper to eggs and beat with fork until blended. Melt butter in skillet, pour in eggs, add crumbled cheese and chives. Cook over low heat, stirring until eggs set but are still moist. Do not overcook!

Carbohydrates: 6 grams, or a little more than 1 per serving

Sunday Breakfast or Brunch
- Tray of juices or drinks such as Bloody Mary, Ramos Gin Fizz, or Champagne
- Fried ham or little sausages
- Eggs Marvelous (see next page)
- Half slices of whole wheat toast, or scones, muffins, or other pastries cut in small serving sizes
- Quarters of peeled cantaloupe, fresh melon balls, or equivalent frozen variety, sugar-free
- Coffee or breakfast tea

As a late breakfast or brunch is really two meals in one, you can afford the relatively high carbohydrate count. If you prefer doughnuts to toast, add 3 grams per serving.

Carbohydrates: 14 per serving, exclusive of preliminary drinks

---

Eggs Marvelous

This version of scrambled eggs is done in a double boiler to make sure the result is not over-cooked.

- 2 tablespoons butter
- 1 tablespoon chopped green onions (scallions)
- 6 eggs
- ⅓ cup light cream
- ¼ teaspoon lemon juice
- 1 3-oz. package cream cheese, crumbled

Melt butter in top of double boiler. Add onions and simmer about five minutes. While they cook, combine eggs, cream, lemon juice, cheese, and salt to taste. Add to onions in double boiler and cook slowly until eggs are barely set—about 10 minutes, usually. Stir occasionally to test. Serves 4.

Carbohydrates: 11 overall, or about 3 per serving

Cheddar Cheese Scramble

To serve three, melt 1 tablespoon butter in skillet, preferably Teflon no-stick. Add ½ cup (2 ounces) diced or sliced well-aged Cheddar cheese, the sharper the better. Beat 4 eggs slightly with 3 tablespoons milk. Add to melted cheese in skillet, season with salt and pepper, and scramble gently until almost firm. Serve immediately on hot plates.

The trick lies in melting the cheese slowly and being ready with the eggs the moment the cheese is melted. And always remember, hot plates!

Keep heat low. There's nothing worse than an overdone egg.

Carbohydrates: 6 grams in the entire dish, or 2 per serving

Ham Scramble

For 4 servings, add a 2¼ oz. can of deviled ham to six eggs and beat together with fork until well mixed. Add 2 tablespoons milk or water. Heat 2 tablespoons butter in large skillet. Pour egg mixture in and cook until just the right consistency. With deviled ham, no further seasonings needed.

Carbohydrates: 5 grams in entire recipe, or barely over 1 per serving

Mushroom Scramble

Cook about ½ cup sliced fresh mushrooms in 2 tablespoons butter, seasoning with salt and pepper. Beat 4 eggs slightly, add 3 tablespoons milk, and pour mixture over mushrooms. Cook gently over low heat until eggs are set. Three servings.

A modern touch: substitute any fresh vegetable for the mushrooms, or any combination, including mushrooms. This "vegetable scramble" has the great advantage or letting the vegetables do the cooking, as the water in them retains their heat. Tomatoes are especially good. Don't hesitate to experiment: add feta cheese or grated Parmesan to complete.

Carbohydrates: for mushrooms, about 3 grams per serving

Oven Omelet

Here you start by separating 6 eggs into whites and yolks, by cracking shells in half, as evenly as possible, with knife, and pouring the whites off into a shallow dish by turning the yolks back and forth from the half shells. The rest of the ingredients are simply water, salt and pepper, and butter.

Turn on over to 350 degrees. Beat egg whites and set aside. With the same beater thoroughly mix the egg yolks with water, salt, and pepper. As the contents of this bowl become foamy, fold the beaten whites into it.

Now melt 2 tablespoons butter in frying pan and pour eggs into it, cooking over low heat into it, but not stirring. As bottom of omelet browns, set skillet into 350-degree oven for a few minutes until puffing begins and top is dry. Slide out onto hot platter. Serves four.

Carbohydrates: less than 1 gram per serving

Spanish Sauce for a 6-egg Omelet

Many breakfast fans gravitate to catsup, hot sauce, or salsa on eggs or omelets. Here's the original version:

1½   tablespoons oil
 3   tablespoons minced onion
 2   tablespoons chopped green pepper, or canned green chiles
 1   cup (8-oz. can) stewed tomatoes

Heat oil in small saucepan and in it cook onion until it is limp. Add other ingredients, season as needed, and heat to boiling. Pour over omelet or scrambled eggs on serving platter, or use sauce to fill omelet.

Carbohydrates: about 4 grams per serving

Shirred Eggs in Stewed Tomatoes

For six servings, heat 1 cup, or 8 oz. can of stewed tomatoes in small saucepan. While it heats, turn oven to 375 degrees and butter six custard cups. Set cups in shallow pan, with an inch or so of hot water in the bottom. Spoon some of the hot tomato into each cup, break an egg in to it, sprinkle with salt and pepper. Bake 12-15 minutes until eggs are firm. Serve in the cups, along with crisp toast.

Carbohydrates: about 2 grams per serving

Bacon and Egg Bowl

Here's a hearty breakfast that's worthy of a comeback!

- 8   eggs
- 4   slices bacon
- 4   green onions (scallions)
- 2   tablespoons butter

Hardboil the eggs exactly 10 minutes in gently boiling, salted water. When eggs are done drop into cold water, but before they cool, shell them and cut up coarsely. Meanwhile, fry bacon until crisp but not over-dry. Take up and crumble. Chop onions fine, including some of the green tops. Heat a quart bowl in oven and add butter. Add all ingredients into this bowl. Toss, salt and pepper to taste, and serve at once.

Carbohydrates: about 2 grams per serving

Egg Foo Yung, or Chinese Omelet

Nowadays they'd call this a fusion dish. But let's treat it as just a nice way to do an omelet:

- 6   eggs
- 1   (15-oz.) can bean sprouts, drained
- 2   tablespoons chopped green pepper
- ½   cup shredded green onion
     Salad oil

Add salt and pepper to eggs, to taste, and beat well. Add sprouts, green pepper, and onion. Form into half cupfuls, or cakes. With a minimum of oil heat a skillet very hot and drop mixture in. Level the tops of the cakes as they cook with a spatula. Flip over to brown both sides. Allow about 5 minutes cooking time. Lift onto warm plates and serve with soy sauce. Makes 6 cakes.

Carbohydrates: 5 grams per cake

Frittata, Italian Vegetable Omelet

There are probably as many recipes for frittata as there are good Italian cooks. In general, the following are the proportions usually followed.

For 3 or 4 servings, allow:

6 eggs, separated

3 cups cooked vegetables, such as spinach, artichoke hearts, zucchini, or green beans

3 tablespoons grated Parmesan cheese

½ teaspoon each of garlic salt and seasoned salt

½ teaspoon mixed herbs, such as oregano, rosemary, parsley, garlic Olive oil

Beat yolks of eggs. Add mix of vegetables, cheese, seasonings. Beat egg whites stiff, and fold into yolk mixture. Heat oil in heavy skillet, pour in the mixture, cook without stirring for a few minutes over moderate heat, then bake at 350 degrees for about 25 minutes, or until firm. Cut into edges and serve from skillet. Frittata is good plain, with spaghetti sauce, hot or cold.

Carbohydrates: about 5 per serving, exclusive of any sauce

Suggested wine: anything Italian, white best with cold frittata. This is mainly to get into the spirit of the occasion

---

Lunchtime Menu of a Traditional Italian

- Frittata, as above
- Bread sticks
- Choice of lettuce with oil and vinegar dressing
- Red-checked tablecloth!

This full lunch can be enjoyed without consuming more than 20 grams of carbohydrates per person. The spirit of the occasion suggests *al fresco* atmosphere (under the trees).

Wine suggestion: a light red, such as Chianti or Grenache Rose, chilled. Served outdoors, the lunch will be easy to serve cold, but the herbs usually require more than a white wine as competition.

Frittata Foo Yung

Here is another fusion opportunity, made easy by the simple substitution of traditional Chinese vegetables for the Italian favorites. The omelet is the same as the preceding Italian Frittata except for canned chop suey and chopped scallions instead of the fresh cooked vegetables. The same baking directions apply, but serve with soy sauce or even hot (red) Chinese sauce.

Carbohydrates: about 4 grams per serving

Eggs Benedict

This all-time classic deserves special attention, as it has become a favorite on any breakfast or brunch menu. Important note: eggs can be poached in advance and held in a skillet of warm (not hot) water, ready for their spot in the assembly line.

> 2   English muffins split crosswise (usually partially split as they come packaged)
> utter enough for the above
> 4   thin slices of cooked ham
> 4   eggs
> Hollandaise sauce (see p. 94)
> Paprika

Toast English muffin halves and butter them lightly. Keep in warm oven until ready to serve, on individual, warmed plates. Warm ham in skillet with a little oil. Poach eggs (as below), noting that this can be done in advance. Now, working quickly, place a slice of ham on each muffin half, on split side, top with a poached egg, and cover with Hollandaise sauce. Sprinkle with Paprika and serve at once.

Carbohydrates: about 11 grams per serving

Perfect Poached Eggs

For four eggs, boil water at least an inch and a half deep in a good-sized skillet. Add 2 tablespoons salt and 1 tablespoon vinegar to help set the whites. Remove skillet from heat, and when water has stopped boiling crack and slip eggs carefully into the hot water. Water will completely cover the eggs. Let stand a minute.

Carefully lift skillet back over heat and allow eggs to cook as firm as you prefer.

Carbohydrates: 1 gram for 2 eggs, a normal serving

Old-Fashioned Deviled Eggs

Good deviled eggs depend to a great extent on just right cooking of the eggs. When done well, they are not just the typical picnic fare, but part of basic French cuisine.

Hard-boil six eggs in a saucepan with enough water to more than cover them. After water reaches a boil, turn down heat to low and cook *well below boiling point* for about 15 minutes. Now cool eggs quickly by dropping them in very cold water. Eggs will peel easily if you have followed this method. Cut eggs in half lengthwise, remove yolks, and mash them with:

- 1 **tablespoon softened butter**
- 3 **tablespoons mayonnaise**
- ¼ **teaspoon seasoned salt**
- 1 **teaspoon prepared mustard**
- 2 **tablespoons white wine vinegar**

Mix thoroughly, adding a little more butter and mayonnaise to taste. Now line up the 12 egg white halves and fill them with the mix. Arrange on platter and garnish with parsley, for help-yourself serving.

Carbohydrates: about ½ gram per egg

For Diablo Deviled eggs, add chili powder or Mexican hot sauce to yolk mixture, and proceed as above. Always start with a little seasoning and add to taste.

For Curried eggs, add 1 teaspoon curry powder and bits of crisply cooked bacon to the above basic yolk mixture. Three slices will be sufficient for a six-egg recipe.

Carbohydrates: not enough additional grams to count

Cheese Souffle

Before beginning the soufflé, generously butter a 1½ quart mold about 4 inches deep, with fairly vertical sides. Heat oven to 400 degrees. Now prepare a sauce with grated cheese:

- 3 **tablespoons butter**
- 3 **tablespoons flour**
  Dash of cayenne pepper
  Dash of nutmeg
- 1 **cup milk**
- 1 **cup (4 oz.) coarsely grated sharp Cheddar**
- 5 **egg yolks**
- 5 **egg whites**

First make a thick cream sauce: Melt butter in a large skillet. Form a paste with flour by gradually adding a little milk to it, then seasonings and finally stirring into butter. Add remaining milk, salt to taste, and cook slowly, stirring, until thick and smooth. Remove from heat.

Beat egg yolks with a fork (save the fifth yolk for another day, for mayonnaise or Hollandaise sauce). Very gradually add yolks to hot mixture, stirring briskly. Add cheese and stir until melted. Remove from heat and set aside.

Beat egg whites very stiff. Now the big secret of a successful soufflé: take only ¼ of the beaten whites and stir briskly into the sauce, mixing thoroughly. Only then, quickly but gently, fold in the remaining whites. *Fold* means just that: do not try to mix thoroughly, or the soufflé will lose its lightness.

Pile this fluffy mixture into the buttered mold, filling about ¾ full. Level the top with a spoon. Set mold on center rack of hot oven, at once turning it down to 375 degrees. Bake undisturbed for 30 minutes. If it is puffed high and well browned, take to table and serve at once. Otherwise, give it a few minutes longer until it appears right. Result: a lovely dish for four persons.

Carbohydrates: 32 grams in entire recipe, or 8 per person

Wine suggestion: Riesling, Liebfraumilch, Champagne

Welsh Rarebit

Another classic, seldom attempted at home, but really not that difficult:

- ½   **tablespoon Worcestershire sauce**
- ⅛   **teaspoon paprika**
- ½   **teaspoon dry mustard**
-     **Dash of cayenne pepper**
- ½   **cup ale (milk may be substituted)**
- 1   **pound sharp Cheddar cheese, crumbled**
-     **Toast, especially wheat or rye**

Mix seasonings to a paste in a heavy saucepan. Stir in liquid, and let simmer over very low heat until mixture is hot. Add the cheese and continue cooking and stirring until cheese is melted. Serve immediately over hot toast.

Carbohydrates: about 3 grams per serving, nor counting toast

Cheese Fondue

A fondue pot, which has a candle or other slow heat source such as Sterno under it, is essential to success in serving. And serving is the thing that separates this dish from any other. Each person will dip into the melted cheese with cubes of bread on fondue forks or skewers, leisurely. If the cheese cools and hardens, the dish is over. When done with care, a fondue is a classy side dish for a party of four to a dozen people.

Shred well-aged Swiss cheese coarsely—imported or American, as you prefer, and from a half pound to two or more, depending on the size of your party and your Fondue pot! Put into casserole or saucepan, and pour a white table wine over it until barely covered. Take your time melting the cheese, as long as 45 minutes over very low heat. Stir frequently to achieve smoothness. Now stir in Kirsch (cherry-flavored brandy) or equivalent, about a tablespoon to a pint of mixture of cheese and wine. Serve without further spices, as above.

Carbohydrate: 1 gram per ounce of cheese. Bread cubes are about another 3 grams per serving size for an ounce of cheese.

Carbohydrate Cut-Downs

In this dairy chapter you've seen how the carbohydrates come mainly from the accompaniments to the cheese or eggs: the toast, the bread sticks, the wonderful green vegetables in frittata, the potatoes on the side of poached eggs. So to keep yourself within the sixty carbohydrates that should be your limit for losing weight, you'll need strategies to avoid the 'deal killers'.

Get in the habit of eating half a potato rather than a whole one, six big home fries rather than twelve, half a bagel instead of the whole thing, half a piece of toast, even. No one will look at you as if you've taken leave of your senses. Get used to the idea of fewer "starchy foods." Your taste buds will soon tell you that's what you like: less.

Try diluting the carbohydrates with foods that contain less than their neighbors. Tomatoes mixed with potatoes or rice. Use more chopped green onions, or scallions, in any breakfast dish with eggs. Slice red or green peppers to replace croutons in salads. A vegetable like zucchini is available almost all year round: slice it mix it in with green beans or peas, fresh or frozen, and cut down on several grams per serving.

Use certain meats and fish as spices rather than main courses. A touch of ham or bacon can turn a green salad into a main dish. Use sliced meat or cheese in party dips instead of crackers or chips.

The lovely thing about the cutting-down approach is that it also accentuates good nutrition. In short, don't eat 'empty calories' such as sugar and white bread and white rice. Don't begin your sit-down lunch with three pieces of French bread. And don't end it with empty calories at the finish: sugary desserts.

You'll be surprised at how quickly your taste buds change their tune, and call you back to good nutrition.

VEGGIES
WITH THE VITAMINS

The focus of the Drinking Man's Diet has always been on *fine tuning:* getting the most from the least. And the Cookbook based on the same diet goes it one better: fine tuning how you stay on the diet. This is especially true of vegetables.

Choosing and using vegetables in new ways is vital. And for a simple reason: vegetables *do* contain a lot of carbohydrates, but they also contain *the majority of the vitamins that sustain life.* You can't live with 'em, and you can't live without 'em! one would conclude. But that's not true: you can strike a bargain.

This chapter is about that bargain. A few rules:

1. Don't fool yourself: second helpings, third helpings, and all the carbohydrate count goes out the window.

2. Casseroles that contain a wide variety of ingredients just won't work in keeping track of your carbs. Such recipes are avoided here.

3. Green, leafy vegetables are the coin of the realm of diet. OK, carrots, cauliflower, leeks, and other non-green vegetables have nutrients all their own. Just concentrate on the greens.

How to Prepare and Cook Artichokes

The Artichoke is really the flower bud of a giant thistle. As it matures, its leaves, or "bracts," begin to open out, and thorny spines appear at their tips. The best and most tender ones have tightly closed heads and no thorns. The Italian type artichoke is long and cone shaped; the French is round with a slightly flattened top.

To prepare, wash thoroughly, pull off two or three rows of outside bottom leaves, cut off the stem flush with the base, and rub all cut surfaces at once with a cut lemon to prevent discoloring. Cut off the top third of each artichoke squarely, using a large knife, and again rub with lemon.

Have ready a saucepan or kettle into which the artichokes will fit just snugly, so they won't float while boiling. (Try them out in the saucepan in advance.) Put the trimmed artichokes in upright, of course, add boiling water to come up to their tops, and a tablespoon of salt for each quart of water. Don't cover the saucepan; instead, do as the French chefs do: lay a doubled piece of cheesecloth over the artichokes, which forces the water to boil up over the artichoke tops. Add a little vinegar.

Boil rapidly for 20 to 35 minutes; chokes vary greatly in how fresh or tough they are. Test for tenderness by pulling out one or two leaves. The chokes are done when leaves pull out easily.

Lift out, drain briefly upside down, and serve hot with melted butter, or cold with a dipping sauce for the tender ends of the leaves. If the chokes are a bit past their prime, or if they are part of an elegant dinner, remove the center fuzzy thistles by scooping out with a tablespoon.

To make stuffed artichoke salads, remove the thistles as above and add a variety of mixtures: well-seasoned shrimp, crab, or tuna with your favorite dressing, or chicken salad with mayonnaise and chopped celery.

Carbohydrates: 5 or 6 grams per medium artichoke, without stuffing

Wine suggestion: a fruity white to balance the tartness

Artichokes Jerusalem

Why this root vegetable was ever called an artichoke is lost in the mists of history. It's closer to a potato, small and knobby, but full of root flavor. Treat it as a potato: pare its surface lightly and boil it in salted water for 15-30 minutes, checking doneness with a sharp knife. Season with butter or oil and pepper.

Carbohydrates: about 4 grams each

Asparagus, Chinese Style

Fresh asparagus is usually cooked after simply breaking off the tougher ends and, for further tenderness, paring the remaining ends. But slicing asparagus diagonally, as in most Chinese recipes, has a lot going for it: it cooks faster, appears larger in a serving, and thus goes father.

For a serving for four, allow one pound. Wash and trim as above, then slice diagonally starting at the head, about 1½ inches long. Spread slices in a large frying pan, add about ¼ inches water, sprinkle with salt or a little soy sauce, and cook quickly: about five minutes from reaching a boil. Watch it! Don't let pan boil dry. Don't overcook: leave crisp and full of color.

For an extra Oriental touch, add thinly sliced mushrooms and onions to the pan at the start.

Carbohydrates: even with the added onions and mushrooms, the average serving will come to little more than 6 grams

Lemon Sauce for Asparagus or Broccoli

This is a simple version of Hollandaise sauce (see p. 94) without, of course, the egg. Simply heat 1 cup of mayonnaise with 4 tablespoons lemon juice in top of a double boiler. Add dry mustard, if you prefer, or cayenne pepper. Serve hot, to spoon over hot asparagus or broccoli.

Carbohydrates: about 9 grams for a full cup of sauce

Green Beans Almondine for Two

For 1½ cups cooked green beans, allow 12-15 blanched almonds. While beans are steaming—the method we prefer for most vegetables—cut the almonds into thin slivers and brown them lightly in a tablespoon of butter over low heat. At serving time, spoon beans onto serving plates and top with the buttered almonds. That's it!

Note that steaming vegetables allows you to keep them warm long after they're done. A little practice and you can let the vegetables continue steaming well after heat is off, without overcooking. And if they seem undercooked just before serving, they can be steamed up again very quickly.

Carbohydrates: 9 grams per these two generous servings, with another 3 grams for the almonds, for a total of 6 grams per serving

Italian Green Beans

This bean is flatter and broader than Kentucky Wonders or other string beans, and has a distinct, buttery flavor. A pound will serve four. Preparation is simple: just wash, trim ends, and cut in diagonal pieces about and inch or so long. About ten minutes before serving, place beans in a large frying pan with water ¼ inch deep. Sprinkle lightly with salt, cover, and cook until tender and still crisp, about 8 minutes. Make sure they don't boil dry, or you'll have that tell-tale burnt taste.

Or, simply steam them, as above. In either case, seasonings are hardly needed.

Carbohydrates: about 5 grams per serving of ¾ cup

Tri-Color Bean Dish

For a change of pace, try this colorful and spicy alternative to the ordinary vegetable.

Frozen or canned yellow wax beans are widely available. Drain the liquid, if any, and mix them in a bowl with: 2 slices canned pimiento, diced; 2 tablespoons chopped green or red pepper; 1 tablespoon chopped red or yellow onion; a little melted butter. Heat gently in a saucepan or skillet, and season with salt and pepper. The peppers and onions remain crisp.

Carbohydrates: about 7 per serving (of four servings)

About Bean Sprouts

Raw bean sprouts once were ordinarily to be found only in Oriental grocery stores, but now are found everywhere. Usually these are sprouts of Mung beans: they are small and pale green in color. Canned bean sprouts are widely available, and can be used in various dishes simply by rinsing them in cold water.

Sprouts are highly nutritious and add flavor to any dish.

To prepare the raw variety, rinse the sprouts in cold water several times, discarding bruised or discolored pieces. Discard any green husks that float or sink in the water. To store overnight, either sprinkle with water or fully cover with water, in closed container. When preparing, cook 3-4 minutes, just long enough to heat thoroughly, in salted water and a dab of butter. They can also be used raw in salads or main dishes.

Soybean sprouts are larger than Mungs, and are yellow in color, and are prepared differently because of their raw-bean flavor. They require 10-20 minutes of cooking.

Carbohydrates: 4 grams per cup; soybean sprouts: 6 grams. After sprouts are cooked, or if canned, double the grams per cup.

Butter-Steamed Green Beans

For best-ever green beans, try this for a serving for four: Take 1 pound beans, wash, pinch off only the stem end of the beans. Slice in 1-inch pieces, or even split lengthwise. Heat 2 tablespoons butter or fresh bacon drippings in a large skillet with a tight fitting cover. Put in the beans, sprinkle with salt and pepper, and add ¼ cup water. Cover and bring to steaming, then turn to low and let cook for 10-15 minutes, until barely tender but still "squeaky" when bit into. Be careful not to let boil dry! Now add ¼ cup light cream, heat up again, and serve. The difference is in the butter and cream!

Use your imagination to spice up the beans, as in the recipe for tri-color beans, p. 80.

Carbohydrates: about 8 grams per serving, mainly in the beans themselves

Fresh Beets

Canned beets are good eating and easy to serve. Even so, it's worthwhile to fix fresh beets occasionally because of the difference in their delicate fresh flavor.

Allow 1 pound, an ordinary bunch of beets, to serve 2-3 people. But why not cook an extra bunch or so, as they can easily be reheated later?

Wash beets; cut off tops, but leave 2 inches of stems so beets won't bleed. Leave the tap root on for the same reason. Cover with water in pot and boil, covered, until tender when tested with a fork—about 30-40 minutes. Remove and rinse in cold water, slipping off the skins, stems, and tails. Beets can then be served in a variety of ways, with a little lemon juice or vinegar to retain color in a salad. They can also be reheated and served warm, with salt, pepper, or other spices.

Carbohydrates: 9 grams for a ½ cup serving

Shoestring Beets on Spinach

In the old days, home-grown young beets were cooked and served with their greens. This recipe hearkens back to that period, using spinach to mimic the greens.

For two servings, take an 8-oz. can of shoestring beets and a 10-oz. package of frozen spinach. You'll need only half the spinach, so wrap and save it. (You can also do this with fresh vegetables, of course; it just takes longer.)

Heat beets slowly in their liquid in a saucepan. Thaw and cook spinach. Drain both vegetables well and season with salt and pepper. Have on hand a hard-boiled egg to slice for garnish. Serve a small mound of spinach on each plate and top with a few beets. A nice touch is vinegar in a cruet, bringing out the flavor of both vegetables.

Carbohydrates: 9 grams per serving

Brussels Sprouts

The "little cabbages" are as good for you as their larger cousins.

One pound of sprouts, coming to about 1 quart, is enough to serve four persons. Choose small ones and slice off the stem endings, removing any loose outer leaves.

To speed cooking, with a sharp knife scribe a cross in the top and bottom of each little cabbage. Boil water, lightly salted, about an inch deep in a frying pan and cook sprouts in it for about 8 minutes. As with all vegetables, don't overcook. Season as you prefer, especially with a dash of vinegar or Paprika, and serve at once. Butter, lemon juice, cream with nutmeg, or lemon-mayonnaise sauce (see p. 79) are also good choices.

Carbohydrates: about 8 grams for a ¾ cup serving

Onion Sour Cream Dressing

Consider this sauce in the middle of the cabbage section: perfect for any hot vegetable, but especially Brussels sprouts or cabbage. Start with ½ cup sour cream, add ½ teaspoon instant minced onion, then 2 tablespoons lemon juice. Season as desired with salt and pepper. Heat gently, avoid boiling.

Carbohydrates: about 5 grams in all, enough for four servings

Broccoli the French Way

Fresh broccoli is at its best September through April: make the most of it. It's nutritious, easy to fix, low in carbohydrates!

Broccoli got a bad name in the old days from over-cooking. Too often it turned out gray, mushy, and off-flavor. Try handling it this way, as the French chefs do:

In the market, look for crisp young broccoli bunches. Avoid ones with yellow flower buds. Buy crowns where available, as you're going to use the thick stalks only minimally.

Wash well in cold water. Pare down the stems right below the branching, ruthlessly peeling off any tough skins. Cut the stalks in halves or quarters, lengthwise, so they will cook as quickly as the tender flowerets.

About ten minutes before serving, bring 5 or 6 quarts of water to boil at a galloping pace in a large kettle, with about 3 tablespoons salt. Place broccoli in a wire salad basket and lower it into the boiling water, allowing it to return to boil and boil uncovered for another 4-6 minutes. Broccoli should be tender but still crisp on testing. Lift out, drain, and serve at once, with rice-wine vinegar, lemon juice, melted butter, Hollandaise sauce, or your favorite sauce.

Done this way, the stalks and all will be bright green, delicate in flavor, and fully inviting. The short time in the boiling water keeps the nutritional value intact. Steaming is, of course, always a good option, and requires far less water.

If part or all of the broccoli is intended for salad use, plunge it into ice-cold water immediately after cooking, then store in a tight container in the refrigerator.

Broccoli can also be cooked in a frying pan in just a low level of water, for 6-8 minutes, where it is easier to watch. About the only thing you can do wrong with broccoli is to overcook it!

Carbohydrates: 6 grams in a normal serving of about ¾ cup

How to Boil Cabbage Till Crisp-Tender

Consider this range of options, from 3 minutes to 25:
- Chinese cabbage, 3-5 minutes
- Shredded green cabbage, 6 minutes
- Older white cabbage, in wedges, 12 minutes
- Shredded red cabbage, as long as 25 minutes

Carbohydrates: 5 grams per 1 cup serving

Skillet Cabbage, Two Ways

Coarsely shred cabbage, about 4 cups, and have ready 1 medium chopped onion, 1 stalk of celery, thinly sliced, and a few strips of green or red pepper.

Season with salt and pepper and heat in skillet with a little butter. Brown all vegetables and then steam, as moisture from vegetables will allow. Stir occasionally. Allow 4-5 minutes.

A second version is to replace the butter with 3 or 4 strips of bacon. When they are crisp, take them up, leaving only a tablespoon of hot fat in the pan. Follow through as above. At serving time, you can then embellish the cabbage with crumbled bacon on top.

Carbohydrate: about 9 grams per serving

Mustard Cabbage Wedges

Here we have a vegetable worthy of a main dish. To serve six, with a single cabbage, try:

- 1 head green cabbage, about 1½ lbs.
- 3 tablespoons butter
- 2 tablespoons prepared mustard
- 1 tablespoon chopped onion
- 1 teaspoon Worcestershire sauce

Cut cabbage into 6 wedges. Remove core and hold leaves together firmly by thrusting a toothpick into each wedge.

Now cook, uncovered, 12 to 15 minutes, or until just barely tender. While cabbage is cooking, melt butter in a small skillet and stir in remaining ingredients. Cook slowly, seasoning with salt and pepper. Arrange cabbage on a hot platter and spoon mustard/onion sauce over each wedge.

For cabbage in a corned beef dinner, omit the seasonings.

Carbohydrates: 5-6 grams per serving

Wine suggestion: This light dish can stand a strong wine, such as Syrah or Merlot

Creamed Cabbage

Here's a serving for three. Shred enough cabbage, coarsely, for 3 cups. Put in a large saucepan, pour in boiling water almost to cover, and sprinkle with salt.

Cover pan and cook until cabbage is tender, but not more than 10 minutes (except for winter types). Drain pan, stir in ¼ cup light cream or milk, plus a tablespoon of melted butter. Add seasonings as you prefer, such as a little dill seed.

Heat piping hot and serve immediately. A vinegar cruet is a nice touch when cabbage is served. Remember that cabbage shrinks in cooking quite a bit, so allow only about ⅔ cup per person.

Carbohydrates: 6 grams per serving

Red Cabbage with Wine

If you think cabbage is just for coleslaw or St. Patrick's Day, try this recipe on for size, to serve four:

- 2 **tablespoons butter**
- 2 **tablespoons minced onion**
- 4 **cups shredded red cabbage**
- 2 **tablespoons brown sugar**
- 4 **tablespoons red table wine**
- 1 **tablespoon vinegar**

Saute onion in butter for 3-4 minutes, then add cabbage. Sprinkle with brown sugar, salt and pepper to taste, and add wine and vinegar.

Cook, covered, on low heat for 20-25 minutes, stirring occasionally.

A pounded round steak, browned quickly in olive oil, goes well with this dish. Cabbage takes the place of potatoes in this meat and potatoes combination.

Carbohydrates: 12-13 per serving, including steak, if part of recipe

Wine suggestion: any hearty red, such as Syrah, Merlot, Cabernet, Pinot Noir

Two Good Ways with Carrots

First: Kraut-Carrot Casserole. To serve two, start with 1 cup of sauerkraut (an 8-oz. can, drained), rinse with cold water, and spread in a small, shallow casserole dish. Shred 1 medium-size carrot, and mix with kraut. Dot top with a little butter and bake in moderate oven (350 degrees) for 20 to 30 minutes. Add two or three tablespoons of white wine for moisture and flavor.

Carbohydrates: the kraut is about 7 grams, the carrots 5, or a total of 6 grams per serving. Serve with pork chops or wieners, which add no carbs.

Second: Glazed Carrots. Choose one medium carrot per serving, scrape, and cut in quarters lengthwise. Cook in skillet, in boiling, salted water, enough to cover, until tender. Remove carrots, empty skillet, and quickly heat bacon drippings or butter in skillet and brown carrots thoroughly. A nice accompaniment for a fish dinner.

Carbohydrates: 5 grams per serving

Wine suggestion: a fruity Chardonnay or light, dryed for either dinner

Carrot-Bean Merger

Carrots and green beans work well together, either fresh or canned. If fresh, the beans with carrots (cut lengthwise in quarters) should be steamed for about 10 minutes, then cut bite-size. Mix with sweet or sour cream and onion salt, with a touch of dill, and serve in small dishes with slices of baguette for dipping.

Carbohydrates: 5 grams per serving, exclusive of bread

Wine suggestion: steamed vegetables usually go well with white wine, the drier the better, so try a Sauvignon Blanc or a simple white table wine with this snack

To Cook Cauliflower

Wash cauliflower head, trim away green leaves, and break into flowerets for quick cooking. A normal head of about one pound will serve two generously and three along with a normal meal. Cook in boiling salted water, about an inch deep, until barely tender—not more than 12 minutes or so. Drain, season with butter and a little milk or half and half. Then reheat just prior to serving. You can also cook the head whole by tying it in cheesecloth or using a steamer—but it will take another ten minutes to cook.

Carbohydrates: about six grams per serving, and an additional gram for the milk or half and half.

Cauliflower and Brussels Sprouts

This combination adds variety for a party of five or six people, cooks the same way as above, and makes a pleasing presentation. Simply add an equal amount of the sprouts, well trimmed.

Carbohydrates: you will increase the carbs about fifty percent by adding brussels sprouts, as they are 12 grams per cup. So a mixed serving would come to about 9 grams.

Corn Notes

Corn seems to be getting sweeter each year: one ear used to be 16 grams of carbohydrates but might now run to 20. Break ears in half and cook only a few minutes in rapidly boiling water. Half ears are easier to arrange on plates and allow the carb-conscious to politely stop at one!

For a South American touch, use a little lime or lemon juice instead of butter when serving, then season with paprika or chili powder.

Carbohydrates: 8-10 grams per half ear, with another gram for the South American seasonings.

Vegetable Plate with Franks

Even though some vegetables are rather high in carbohydrates, when vegetables are in season there's nothing like combining them for a great summer dinner. Here's one pleasing combination:
- Half ears of buttered corn
- Green beans served with crumbled, crisp bacon
- Skillet-browned frankfurters (allow 2 per serving)
- Cucumbers, tomatoes and seafood salad
- Hot or iced tea

Carbohydrates: about 20 grams per serving

This Eggplant Casserole is Wonderful with Lamb

When you put this gorgeous color combination of purple, red, and white together you'll think you have enough food for seven or eight. However, the vegetables shrink in cooking, so it comes out right for four hungry people. You'll need:

1	medium-size eggplant (about 1½ lb.)
1	white onion, sliced or coarsely chopped
2	large or 3 small tomatoes
1	green pepper
	butter, salt, pepper
	Oregano, thyme, sweet basil or other herbs

Peel eggplant as needed (see next page) and cut into small cubes of an inch or more. Spread these in a buttered casserole and sprinkle with salt and pepper. Scatter a layer of onion over this, and dot with strips of green pepper and thin slices of tomato. Season with herbs and further salt and pepper as needed. Add dots of butter and a few tablespoons of water, cover, and bake at 350 degrees for at least 30 minutes. Check occasionally for tenderness.

Carbohydrates: about 56 grams, or 14 per person

Wine suggestion: with a leg of lamb, a bold white will work as well as a Grenache Rose or light red, such as a Rhone

---

Summer Dinner Featuring Eggplant

- Eggplant casserole, as above
- Broiled lamb chops, 2 small ones per person
- Skillet-browned slices of liverwurst
- Rye crisp
- Romaine lettuce with oil and vinegar
- Coffee

Serve meats on heated plates, leaving space for eggplant, to be served at table. Serve torn lettuce leaves in small bowls, with oil and vinegar cruets on the side. Serve Rye crisp in a small basket. You will be pleased with how the liverwurst goes with the lamb.

Carbohydrates: About 25 grams per serving. Go easy on the mint jelly with the lamb!

To Prepare and Cook Eggplant

If the purple skin is shiny and you can puncture it easily with your thumbnail, the eggplant is really fresh and you do not need to peel it. On the other hand, if the skin looks dull, better pare off at least part of the peel.

One good way to fix eggplant is to slice it crosswise and broil lightly on both sides, brushing with oil, and seasoning with salt and pepper. Or you can brown slices quickly in a little butter and oil in a skillet. Or you can cut eggplant into small chunks and cook them in a small amount of boiling water until tender. In all three cases, a good way to serve them is with stewed tomatoes, seasoned with your choice of herbs. A 1-lb. eggplant will easily serve four.

Carbohydrates: there are about 5 grams per serving from one large eggplant as cooked above.

Fried Okra with Tomatoes

Notice how tomatoes work well with almost any other vegetable. That's because of their high acidity and the way their liquid content preserves heat. For two servings of okra, start with 16 pods or so. Wash, snap off the stem ends, and cut in thick slices crosswise. Chop a small onion and simmer in a pan; add okra and cook, covered, until tender. Add an 8-oz. can of tomatoes and continue cooking until very hot.

Carbohydrates: about 15 grams per serving

Glazed Onions

Drain a 1-lb. can of small Dutch onions. In a skillet heat ¼ cup white wine, 1 tablespoon sugar, and 2 tablespoons butter. Add onions and heat, stirring, until onions take on a deep sun-tan shade—about ten minutes. The result is a good vegetable to go with broiled fish. There are about six small servings here, or 4-5 onions each.

Carbohydrates: 48 in all, or 8 per serving

Peas with Mushrooms and Onions

Another pleasing combination, and easy to fix. For a serving for four, begin with 1 small onion, thinly sliced and sauteed in butter. Add ½ cup thinly sliced mushrooms, then 10-oz. package frozen peas with a little water and salt. Cover and cook for 5 or so minutes, stirring occasionally.

Mushrooms and onions improve just about everything!

Carbohydrates: 8 grams per serving

About Peppers

Don't overlook bell peppers, pimiento and green chili peppers as vegetables in themselves rather than seasons or salad fixings. Early in the summer the skin on these peppers is too delicate to remove successfully. All you have to do is wash them, cut the stems out along with the seed core, and drop them into boiling water for a few minutes, until wilted.

Drain, drop into cold water, drain again, then fry or stuff, as you wish. Later in the season, when the skin has toughened, you'll have to peel them before cooking. To do this, put the peppers under the broiler and turn the peppers frequently until the skin is well blistered. At once put them into a paper bag, close, and let stand for 15 minutes to steam. Then peel.

For a colorful, zippy relish, skin and scald fresh sweet pimiento or green bell peppers, or some of each, take out the seeds, and cut peppers into strips. Rub a bowl with garlic, put in the pepper strips, and add oil, red wine vinegar, and salt and pepper to taste. Cover and refrigerate at least two hours.

These peppers will keep fresh for about two weeks if refrigerated. They can be used in a variety of salads and hot dishes.

Carbohydrates: The average green pepper contains about 3 grams; a red pepper slightly more

Summer Squash Story

Sizes of summer squash vary considerably across the country and from season to season. A general rule is to allow, for each serving, one or two small, pale green "patty pans," or a 5- to 6-inch long dark green zucchini, or a little yellow crook-neck. One zucchini that length makes about ¾ cup sliced raw, or ½ cup after cooking.

Whatever the variety, just wash and trim, but do not pare. Cut or dice as you like, and cook briefly, 7-10 minutes. Then season and serve.

During summer, when there is a big supply of squash in the market, it's fun to pick up one or two of each variety and mix them into a medley. They all take the same amount of time to cook.

Carbohydrates: about 8 grams per cupful of cooked squash. (A cup obviously holds more squash the finer it's cut up.)

Zucchini with Zip

Start with about ½ pound zucchini, thinly sliced. Slice a small onion and saute in olive oil until translucent; add zucchini. Garlic salt, a dash of Worcestershire sauce or Tabasco, and a little water does the rest. Cooking time is only 8 minutes or less, and you have the perfect accompaniment to a hamburger. This recipe serves two.

Carbohydrates: about 9 grams per serving

Summer Squash with Bacon

A pound of summer squash, of any variety, will yield about four servings. Wash but don't peel (the vitamins are in the skin, as our grandmothers used to say). Cut into good-size slices or cubes and cook, covered, in a small amount of boiling, salted water—better yet, *steam* them over that water in a metal basket and don't lose the vitamins in the water.

During cooking, about 10 minutes or less, fry 4 slices thinly sliced bacon, pour off most of the fat, and sauté ¼ cup chopped onions in the remaining fat. When squash is done, namely, not mushy but barely allowing a fork to pierce it, place in serving dish and pour crumbled bacon and onions over. No further seasoning needed!

Carbohydrates: about 8 grams per serving

Crunchy Spinach

This recipe combines two low-carb vegetables, spinach and celery. A pound of fresh spinach, a large bunch, and a thinly sliced cup of celery will yield about three servings. Wash spinach first in warm water, cut off the stems, and wash again in cold water. (Spinach is one of the most difficult vegetables to get thoroughly clean of grains of sand, so a third washing is often needed. You want the crunch in the celery!)

Steam the spinach—it will become limp in only a few minutes—and meanwhile cook the celery in a little oil. Cut through spinach with a kitchen knife and drain. With celery, add 1 or 2 tablespoons cream and similar amount of prepared horseradish.

Carbohydrates: about 6 grams per serving

Spinach Supreme

You can make this simple recipe with either frozen or fresh spinach—a 10-oz package of the former or a bunch of the latter. It's so easy you can remember it just by checking your refrigerator—for some sour cream and grated cheese, preferably Cheddar or Parmesan.

Steam the fresh spinach or cook the frozen as directed on the package. Be sure to cut the cooked leaves down to bite size. Then just stir in a couple tablespoons sour cream and grate the cheese over it all. Heat before serving, and season as desired. Serves three comfortably.

Carbohydrates: less than 3 grams per serving

Broiled Tomatoes, Simple

When tomatoes are in season, this is a crowd-pleaser. Select about a dozen small to medium tomatoes for a serving for four. Cut each in half crosswise and arrange cut-side up on a baking pan. Now use your imagination: drizzle some oil with salt and pepper over them, or add some grated cheese, or even bread crumbs. Place under a medium broiler for just a few minutes. Turn off broiler and serve as soon as possible.

Carbohydrates: only 3 grams per serving

Broiled Tomatoes, Parmesan

Follow the same recipe as above, but with special attention to herbs and cheese. For Parmesan, a teaspoon of oregano works well. With tomatoes at the peak of the season, this can be a main course: use larger tomatoes, and slice in thirds instead of halves.

The difference now is that you can serve these on trimmed toast, on hot plates, with a simple garnish such as lettuce and pickles or thinly sliced red onions.

Carbohydrates: only 3-4 grams per serving

Sauces for Vegetables

Good seasoning for any vegetable starts with good cooking. And that means not *overcooking*. If you have managed so that only a spoonful or two or liquid is left in the pan when you've cooked vegetables in water, you don't have to worry about seasoning. A dash of pepper or paprika will do. The natural flavor of perfectly cooked vegetables is wonderful.

If you demand it, and your weight can stand it, please add a little butter or cream to the vegetable, just before serving. And when you're in the mood for a special sauce, you may like to indulge in one of these:

Vinaigrette Sauce

- ½ cup olive oil, or equivalent
- ¼ cup tarragon vinegar
- 1 teaspoon salt
- ¼ teaspoon paprika
- 1 tablespoon chopped chives or onion
- 1 tablespoon chopped parsley
- ¼ teaspoon sugar
- 1 slice canned pimiento, finely chopped

Blend ingredients together in top of double boiler and warm over hot, not boiling water. Yield: about ¾ cup, enough for most salads or over such veggies as asparagus or 'patty pan' squash, with a colorful appearance.

Carbohydrates: 7 in all, or less than 2 in usual serving

Standard Recipe for Hollandaise

½   **cup butter (1 stick)**
2   **egg yolks, unbeaten**
1   **tablespoon lemon juice, or vinegar**
    Dash of Cayenne pepper

Divide the butter into three equal parts, so that you can add the latter two during cooking. You can use a double boiler, but a simpler stovetop method works well—as long as you never allow the skillet to become too hot! French chefs typically hold the side of the frying pan to test this heat.

Melt the first third of butter in a skillet and gradually stir in egg yolks and sprinkle with cayenne pepper. When mixture is smoothly thickened, add lemon juice/vinegar to 'fix' the mixture. Then gradually add the second and third parts of the butter, stirring constantly. Salt and pepper as needed.

You may also add herbs to the butter before adding egg yolks—including finely diced scallions.

Don't reheat, but extend the sauce, as needed with more butter. If curdling occurs, stir in a tablespoon of boiling water and whip vigorously until smooth. This is a traditional sauce for asparagus, broccoli, or artichokes, about ½ cup in all, or enough for 3-4 servings.

You can also make a **'mock' Hollandaise** with mayonnaise and a half amount of sour cream, heating over hot water.

Carbohydrates: 2 grams for standard recipe, per total; somewhat under 7 grams for Mock Hollandaise

Spur-of-the-Moment Sauces

Mustard-catsup sauce: Mix equal parts prepared mustard and tomato catsup—a good dip for fried shrimp and a touch of flavor for such vegetables as artichoke hearts or cabbage.

Carbohydrates: about 3 grams per tablespoon

Mustard-Cream Sauce: Stir 2 tablespoons prepared mustard into ⅓ cup heavy cream in small sauce pan. Add 1 tablespoon butter and heat until melted. Excellent for cabbage, broccoli, or cauliflower and enough for four servings.

Carbohydrates: Practically none

Browned butter with herbs: In a small skillet heat 4 tablespoons butter until golden brown. Add 1-2 tablespoons minced fresh herbs, such as thyme, savory, marjoram, oregano, or rosemary. Serve on green beans, Brussels sprouts, spinach, snap peas.

Carbohydrates: None in this ultimately simple sauce

7
STAYING FRESH
WITH SALADS

Part of the pleasure of salad making lies in going creative: adding out-of-the-ordinary seasonings. Or mixing unexpected ingredients together. Or serving the salad in some slightly different way. So go ahead and do just that. But do keep in mind how many grams of carbohydrates you are tossing together. If in doubt, check with the tables given at the end of this book.

Such hearty 'bowl' salads as bean, potato, and macaroni salads do contain a good many carbohydrates, and this is fine for active persons who have no weight problems. For weight watchers, the servings should be small. Half a cup of kidney bean salad, for example, contributes more than 21 grams of carbs. Most potato salads can easily add up to 30 grams per normal serving. And a lesser amount of macaroni salad can run even higher.

The salads and dressings presented here are sensible as to carbohydrate count, and mighty good eating, too. So tuck them away mentally for future experimentation. Keep the rest of your carbs in check, and serve these with a flourish!

The Lettuce Bowl

To make an oil and vinegar dressing for the lettuce, the traditional way, proceed something like this—but don't be timid with your own ideas.

For four generous servings, break or tear crisp lettuce, any variety or a mixture, into a garlic-rubbed bowl. A full head of romaine, butter, or green leafy lettuce is enough, and even too much at the height of the season. Be sure to wash thoroughly, even if it's the packaged variety now so common. Drizzle 3 or 4 tablespoons of olive oil over the torn lettuce, in a large serving bowl. Sprinkle lightly with salt and coarse black pepper and toss until leaves are well coated. If more seasoning is needed—and it will be—chop 3 or 4 green onions (or scallions) and toss in with other herbs, such as dill weed, thyme, or sweet basil. Add seasoned or garlic salt to taste. Now, just before serving, sprinkle on some white wine vinegar and toss again. (If you mix the oil and vinegar in advance, the proportions are about 3-1, and you can add a touch of sugar and dry mustard at that time.)

Carbohydrates: about 4-5 per serving

Semi-Formal Lettuce Salad

Many hostesses like to serve a small green salad on individual plates, presented on the dining table before guests sit down. In this case, do not tear or cut the leaves, but be sure to coat them very lightly with the dressing of your choice. You don't want them wilting, and you can serve a small cruet of dressing on the side. Garnish with a few slices of raw mushrooms, thinly shaved red onions, or tomatoes in season, also coated with dressing.

Salt and pepper very lightly.

Carbohydrates: less than 5 grams per serving, even with tomatoes

Caesar Salad, the Classic

Though this popular salad is higher in carbohydrates than most of the others given in this chapter, it is substantial enough to make a full meal accompanying a small streak or chop—neither of which have carbohydrates. For four good-sized servings you will need:

1 or 2	peeled cloves of garlic
2	tablespoons butter
8	slices Melba toast (about 1 oz.)
1	egg, 'coddled' 1 minute
1	large head romaine lettuce
¼	cup olive oil
	Garlic salt
	Worcestershire sauce
	Black pepper, fresh ground
½	cup grated Parmesan cheese
½	lemon, juice and pulp
2-4	anchovy fillets, cut small

Mash garlic or squeeze through press, mix with butter, and spread on toast slices. Heat briefly, butter side down in hot skillet, to keep firm. Set aside. (Croutons will also do, but it's better to make your own this way.)

Break lettuce into a large salad bowl and coat with olive oil thoroughly. Add seasonings. (You may also with to experiment with other dressings—they are ubiquitous on the shelves of supermarkets—but the difference is usually a matter of herbs, which are readily available fresh.)

When ready to serve, cook the egg for 1 minute in boiling water, sprinkle Parmesan cheese onto the lettuce, and break the egg over the cheese. Quickly add lemon and chopped anchovies. (Anchovy paste can be substituted, mixed with olive oil, but the real thing is always better.) Toss well until no trace of egg is visible.

Break the toast into small pieces and scatter over all. Serve at once and enjoy the classic!

Carbohydrate: about 10 grams per serving

Lettuce Slices or Wedges

For an easy to do salad for four, start with a small head of Iceberg lettuce. Wash thoroughly, remove outside leaves, and cut into 4 crosswise slices, or 4 lengthwise wedges. Place on individual plates and top each wedge or slice with a generous spoonful of "bumpy" dressing.

The "bumps" are sliced celery, chopped green onion, and hard-cooked eggs sliced up. Mix a little mayonnaise with these and add any other seasoning to your taste: even curry powder or chili sauce. Cap the serving off with anything you have on hand: a stuffed olive, some capers, or a cherry tomato.

Armenian Spinach Salad

When spinach comes on the market from local producers, this is a cue to try this salad. For 6 servings you will need:

- 1 lb. spinach
- ½ teaspoon chili powder
- ½ cup chopped onion
- 2 hard-cooked eggs, coarsely chopped
- ¾ cup garlic-seasoned French dressing
- 6 crisp-cooked bacon slices, crumbled

Wash the spinach thoroughly, first in warm water then in cold. Remove stems and tear leaves into bite-size pieces. Drain and sprinkle with chili powder. To greens in bowl add onion, eggs, and dressing (choose any style you prefer). Mix lightly, then sprinkle with bacon bits over all. Serve on individual plates or in bowls. Add a touch of sesame oil for additional flavor.

Carbohydrates: about 5 grams per serving

Wine suggestion: Even a light salad can handle a wine, as dry a white as possible so as not to fight the dressing

Green Bean Salad, Three Ways

1. Drain one 1-lb. can of uncut, French-style green beans. Empty into a shallow bowl and drizzle over them ¼ cup garlic French dressing. Chill for several hours. At serving time, arrange on lettuce leaves and sprinkle generously with grated Parmesan cheese. Makes four servings.

Carbohydrates: about 6 grams per serving

2. Make the bean salad as described above. Then, at serving time, spread out 4 thin slices of thuringer, bratwurst, salami, or other ready-to-eat sausage. Arrange a few beans on each slice, then roll or fold meat over the beans and fasten with a skewer or toothpick to make a simple bundle. This simple dish is nutritious and attractive, and goes well with an omelet or cheese-scrambled eggs.

Carbohydrates: virtually the same as above: 6 grams

3. To serve two in a hurry, drain an 8-oz. can of Blue Lake green beans and place in a small bowl. Cut canned pimientos (2) into strips and stir with a little mayonnaise into beans. Dash with seasoned salt or a little chili powder. Serve over lettuce or alone.

Carbohydrates: again, about the same as above: 6 grams

Cottage Cheese Bowl

For three servings, tear half a head of lettuce of your choice into a garlic-rubbed salad bowl. Make a dressing of 1 cup, or ½ pint, small curd cottage cheese, mixed with a little mayonnaise, some horseradish, chopped onions, and salt and pepper. Mix with lettuce and serve with a slice of rye bread, just the right touch for cottage cheese.

Carbohydrates: 4 grams per serving, plus 11 grams per each slice of rye.

Impromptu Luncheon

- Slices of canned corned beef, chilled for easy slicing
- Dilly toast sticks (see p. 120)
- Cottage cheese sprinkled with chunks of carrot, cucumber, or dill pickle
- Centerpiece of fortune cookies
- Hot Tea

Arrange everything but fortune cookies on individual small plates. Impale the cookies on bamboo sticks of varying lengths and stand them in a heavy mug as a decoration and dessert.

Carbohydrates: 20 grams per serving — depending on the toast!

Celery Victor

This classic is easy to make and easily serves four. A lunch-time centerpiece, it can use some crisp baguette rounds with soft cheese to complete the picture. Here's the basic idea of this famous treat:

1   can hearts of celery (about 1 lb.)
6   tablespoons olive oil
1   tablespoon tarragon vinegar
1   tablespoon cider or wine vinegar
1   tablespoon finely chopped parsley
1   tablespoon chopped dill pickle
    Dash of paprika
    Canned anchovies, a few thin strips

Chill can of celery hearts thoroughly. Mix oil, vinegar, parsley, and chopped pickle together to complete the dressing. At serving time, open can of celery and drain well. Arrange 2 or 3 celery stalks on individual salad plates. Spoon dressing over each, and dash with paprika and thin slices of anchovy.

Yes, fresh celery can be used in this recipe, but it must be thin and well marinated.

Carbohydrates: about 3 grams per serving

Cabbage Salad Bowl

The first step to a good cabbage salad is to use only the tender top half of the head, shredding it fairly fine, and saving the coarser lower half to cook another day. So cut the cabbage head in two crosswise, and after shredding mix it with a mixture of diced cucumber, chopped green pepper, and the usual seasonings of onion salt, paprika, and dill seed.

For the dressing, mix 2 tablespoons vinegar and 1 teaspoon prepared mustard with ½ cup mayonnaise. Stir this over the cabbage and serve.

This salad goes well with ham. To add a nice touch, make lettuce cups and serve individually in the cups.

Carbohydrates: about 5 grams per serving

Crunchy Tuna Salad

For a tray luncheon or for a supper, this salad can hold its own, especially with the wider variety of first-rate canned tuna these days. For four people you will need:

- ½   head lettuce, washed, drained, chilled
- 7   hard-cooked eggs, sliced
- 1   cucumber, pared and sliced
- ¼   cup chopped onion
- 1   7-oz. can tuna, solid, drained and flaked
    French dressing (about ¼ cup)

7 or 8 corn chips or potato chips

Separate lettuce and select 4 cup-shaped leaves to hold the individual salads. Tear remaining lettuce into garlic-rubbed bowl. Add eggs, cucumber, onion, and tuna. Pour dressing over all. Just before serving, crumble the corn chips or potato chips into the bowl, and toss again, serving into the lettuce cups.

Carbohydrates: 8 grams per serving

Vegetable Salad Vinaigrette

There are any number of recipes for Vinaigrette sauce, but all are variations on the main theme. The basic idea can be told in these three ideas:

Use mainly on soft-textured, cooked or canned vegetables such as these: asparagus, bean sprouts, cauliflower, green beans, yellow wax beans, or zucchini (form counts!).

Marinate the vegetables in well-seasoned French dressing (generally, oil and vinegar), and refrigerate at least an hour before serving.

Serve with flair: place on small plate or a platter, but be sure to present with some extras. These could be chopped parsley, finely shopped green onions, pimento, or even hard-cooked, crumbled egg yolks. Use the imagination!

Carbohydrates: Assume the recommended vegetables are eaten in moderation: these are the only carbs. As a rule of thumb there will be about 6 grams in a small serving.

Salmon Salad Platter

Imagine a cookbook that would start here with "Drain a can of... But that was exactly the idea when this cookbook was first written some forty years ago. Nowadays, frozen fish has much to recommend it even over fresh caught. And not just in cost: salmon now frozen on board fishing boats may come to market in a more flavorful way than fresh salmon that has had to run the gauntlet of wholesalers and distributors.

Whatever way you buy salmon, whether steaks or filets, about 1 lb. for six servings, steam or poach it for this recipe, then thoroughly bone and skin it. Break it into large chunks and marinate it in refrigerator, covered, with any well-seasoned dressing, such as French or blue cheese.

For serving, fill a platter with watercress or any shredded lettuce and mound the salmon on top. Garnish the dish with halves of hard-cooked eggs and cherry tomatoes, or wedges. As the salmon is already somewhat dressed, simply serve with a small dish of your favorite dressing.

Carbohydrates: only 5 per serving including garnishes and dressings

Wine suggestion: a perfect dish for a full-bodied Chardonnay

Chicken or Turkey Salad

Another standard, and easy: start with a half cup each of thinly sliced celery, carrots, and walnuts or almonds toasted in butter. Mix a cup and a half of diced cooked chicken or turkey with a half cup mayonnaise and some lemon juice, salt, and pepper.

Combine and serve six scoops onto six cups of Boston lettuce leaves. Garnish with radish slices. Six servings, or four for those with hearty appetites.

Alternative: add sliced green onions and dried cranberries, and a vinai-grette dressing with blue cheese chunks instead of mayonnaise. In either salad, you may also add chopped lettuce to the chicken mixture, and serve without the lettuce cups.

Carbohydrates: about 4 grams per single scoop serving

Wine suggestion: Gewurztraminer, Rhine

Cabbage and Cucumber in Tomato Aspic

This is a little more ambitious, but well worth the effort as something quite out of the ordinary.

2	cups canned tomatoes
½	bay leaf
1	stalk celery
1	envelope plain gelatin
¼	cup cold water
2	tablespoons minced onion
1	tablespoon lemon juice
1	cup finely shredded cabbage
½	cup finely chopped pared cucumber
	Salt, garlic salt, pepper to taste

Simmer together slowly the tomatoes, bay leaf, and celery, lightly salted, until celery is tender. Force all through a strainer. Soften gelatin in cold water for 5 minutes, then add to above mixture until dissolved. Cool.

Add onion, lemon juice, and seasonings. Chill until thick and syrupy. Add cabbage and cucumber. Pour into individual molds and chill until firm. Remove from molds with a little pressure on the bottom and serve on lettuce leaves with a dash of mayonnaise on top each.

This goes well with cold cuts or most seafood.

Carbohydrates: 5 grams per serving

Wine suggestion: Sauvignon blanc, Sancerre

Cukes and Zukes in Sour Cream

Take a cucumber and a zucchini of equal size, pare the 'cuke' and thinly slice both crosswise. Marinate in refrigerator with salt, pepper, minced onions, 1 cup sour cream, and 1 tablespoon lemon juice. This will make 4 or 4 servings, presented in a shallow salad bowl.

Carbohydrates: about 5 per serving

Salad Dressings to Suit Every Taste

Considering the variety of good salad dressings on the shelves of every food market, one might think it's easy to spice up any salad with just a random choice. But read the ingredients: there's a chemical feast out there.

So get in the habit of mixing your own dressings. This way you'll avoid a lot of sugar, in the form of corn syrup. And for a special occasion there's nothing like your own twist. Here are the basics of the favorites. Start here, then experiment:

Classic French

Start with a blend of garden herbs and seasonings: a little fresh rosemary, thyme, marjoram, parsley, for example, added to dry mustard, salt, and pepper. Stir in your best virgin olive oil, ½ cup, 2-3 tablespoons wine vinegar, and 2 teaspoons grated onion. Whisk well. Try a dash of sugar for a little texture, and whisk in well. Let rest in refrigerator with a peeled clove of garlic, then rub the clove around the salad bowl before serving.

Carbohydrates: less than a gram per a tablespoon, a normal serving

Thousand Island

This old standard has gone out of fashion in some quarters, because of its commercialization. But it's still a mighty good addition to vegetable or seafood salads.

- ½ cup mayonnaise
- 2 tablespoons catsup
- 6 stuffed olives, chopped
- 2 green onions, sliced
- 1 teaspoon minced parsley
- 2 hard-cooked eggs, chopped
- ¼ cup heavy cream, whipped
    Salt, pepper, paprika

Mix all ingredients in bowl, adding cream and seasonings, to taste, last. This adds up to about 1½ cups, and is a very rich dressing for even the most flavorful of salads. One tablespoon will do for most servings, hence:

Carbohydrates: 18 grams total, or about 1 gram per tablespoon

Blue Cheese Dressing

Ever notice how often these days, when presented with a choice, most restaurant goers will opt for blue cheese dressing? This seems to be because most of these dressings tend to be cream-based. Here is a classic style:

For a cup of dressing, mash about ⅓ cup blue cheese in a bowl. Add ½ cup olive oil and stir well, gradually adding 3 tablespoons wine vinegar. Beat until smooth, but allowing for a little texture of lumps of cheese. Add salt, celery salt, and pepper to taste.

This simple dressing is great for cantaloupe slices or other fruit salads, as well as on a mixed green.

Carbohydrates: 4 grams in all

Red Wine Dressing

When tomatoes are in season, here's the perfect complement: For 1½ cups, start with ½ cup red wine, ¼ cup red wine vinegar, ¾ cup olive oil. Mix well and season with salt and pepper to taste. Alternatively, pour all ingredients into a bottle with tight lid and simply shake well!

Carbohydrates: 3 grams in all

Yogurt Dressing

- 1 **cup plain yogurt**
- 1 **tablespoon minced onion**
- 2 **tablespoons vinegar**
- ¼ **teaspoon sugar**
  Salt and pepper to taste

Mix all ingredients well and refrigerate until ready to use. Note the lack of oil, the mainstay of dressings. This is a pleasant change from heavy dressings, and works especially well on vegetables, such as cabbage slaw.

Carbohydrates: 16 grams in all, or about 1 gram per the usual serving of a tablespoon

Green Goddess Dressing

Here's our final "classic" dressing, and still a very popular one. The green comes from the chives, green onions, and parsley:

1	clove garlic, grated
2	tablespoons finely chopped anchovies (or 1 tablespoon anchovy paste)
3	tablespoons finely chopped chives or green onions
1	tablespoon lemon juice
3	tablespoons tarragon wine vinegar
½	cup sour cream
1	cup mayonnaise
⅓	cup finely chopped parsley
	Salt and coarse black pepper to taste

Combine ingredients in order above. Chill and hold an hour before use. This results in about 1 pint, enough for 8-12 servings.

Use liberally over mixed greens, with flakes of crab, tuna, or other seafood, as desired. As with most dressings, coat all salad ingredients with dressing before serving on individual plates or bowls. Dressings "on the side" seldom work well.

Carbohydrates: about 18 grams in all, or a little more than a gram per serving

Some Tips About Handling Lettuce

Wash various forms of lettuce the same way—whether romaine, Boston (or butter), Bibb, limestone, or head. That is, as soon as you bring it into the kitchen, remove any wilted leaves but keep the head intact. Dip fully into water, shake out, then drain upside down. Put intact into plastic bag and refrigerate. When ready to make salad, pat each leaf down with paper towel or shake vigorously to remove all moisture possible.

Head lettuce is an old favorite, usually quite crisp, but without the green look of better nutrition. Quite popular nowadays are salad mixes, including arugula, baby spinach, escarole, etc. These should be washed and used as soon as possible. Always remember, fresh is best—but wash!

8
"GET WELL" SOUPS

When you are carbohydrate conscious, and trying to stay at about 60 grams per day, you get in the habit of scrutinizing all foods and all food categories. A look at soups quickly tells you that, since most meats are free from carbohydrates, the broth made from them is also free.

And so, when you make beef stock or chicken broth or buy either of these in cans, you have no carbohydrates to count. But when you add vegetables or noodles or rice to that stock, the soup becomes carbohydratic—if there is such a word! Minestrone, for example, starts with broth. If 2 or 3 cupfuls of vegetables are added, the carbohydrates build up. When cooked navy beans and/or macaroni shells go in also, a big flat bowl of minestrone becomes quite a carbohydrate hazard.

But soups are generally so good for you, distilling all the vitamins from vegetables and all the minerals from bones, that you can't pass them up. After all, chicken soup deserves its restorative reputation! In the recipes that follow, you will see good nutrition along with delectable eating and interesting serving.

To Make Really Good Soup Stock

For beef stock, (bouillon), a meaty beef shank weighing 3 to 4 pounds, sawed into short lengths, is a good choice. If you want the stock brown, cut off part of the meat and brown it in the soup kettle in a little marrow from the bones. For white stock, use a knuckle of veal instead of beef shank, and don't brown it.

When you want chicken broth but are not making a fricassee, buy some chicken backs and necks, plus perhaps a few wings. As you know, you can find these at most big markets at relatively low prices.

For Consommé, use half beef, half veal, plus uncooked bony chicken pieces or bones from cooked chicken.

Starting, then, with 3-4 lbs. meat and bones, cover them with about 3 quarts cold water. Slice and add a small onion, a carrot, and an outer stalk of celery or a handful of leafy tops. Add also a few sprigs of parsley, 1 or 2 bay leaves, 8 or 10 peppercorns, and 2 tablespoons salt. Heat to boiling, skim off obvious fat, then turn heat low and simmer, loosely covered, for 3 hours or longer. Strain, and cool quickly, uncovered. (Soup, like beans, is likely to sour, if the cover is left on while cooling.) Chill, then lift off the fat. This makes about 2 quarts of broth, which you can season further and serve hot as plain broth, or use as the foundation of vegetable soup, onion soup, or other variety.

French Onion Soup

This classic begins with home-made bouillon, as above, or cubes, and depends greatly on the quality of the accompanying French bread:

- 5   medium-sized onions, sliced
- 4   tablespoons butter, or butter and oil
- 5   cups bouillon, or 6 cubes with same water
- 1   teaspoon Worcestershire sauce
- 2   thin slices French bread, toasted and buttered
      Grated Parmesan cheese
      Salt and pepper to taste
      Sherry, as desired

Cook onions gently in butter until golden, sprinkling with pepper while cooking. Add bouillon, sherry, Worcertershire, cover, and simmer 20-30 minutes or until onions are quite tender. Pour into large casserole. Cut each buttered toast slice into thirds and float these on top soup. Sprinkle toast quickly with cheese and bake in top of hot oven (450 degrees) about 10 minutes, until cheese begins to brown. This makes six servings.

Carbohydrates: about 14 grams per serving (toast and onions!)

Sopa Albondigas (Mexican Meatball Soup)

Truly a hearty soup, a complete meal, but low in carbs!

1	onion, minced
1	clove garlic, mashed
¼	cup olive oil
½	cup tomato sauce
2	quarts beef stock
	Sprig of fresh basilica (sweet basil)
½	lb. ground beef
½	lb. ground pork
3	tablespoons raw rice
1	egg, slightly beaten
	Salt and pepper to taste

In large, heavy saucepan, with lid, heat oil and cook onion and garlic until soft. Add tomato sauce and stock, let boil gently while you form small meatballs, by mixing meat with rice, egg, salt and pepper. Drop these into boiling broth, cover tightly, and cook for 30 minutes. Add sweet basil or dash of paprika about 10 minutes before soup is done. Serves 6.

Carbohydrates: about 5 grams per serving

Wine suggestion: Burgundy, hearty table red

Soup and Salad Supper, Mildly Mexican

The Soup: Meatball soup, as above. This is more interesting and easier to eat when served in small bowls.

The Salad: Start with an avocado half and fill with shrimp or crab; flank with 2 deviled eggs, diablo (see p. 73) and a tomato wedge, over chopped lettuce

The Dessert: Orange sections, sprinkled with cinnamon, on small plate

Accompaniment: Piping hot tortillas embellish the soup course, and a 5-inch tortilla has less than 5 grams of carbohydrate

Carbohydrates, including above: 18 grams per serving

Avocado Bouillon

So rich, yet so low in carbs, and so easy to fix: the avocado almost seems an after-thought. To serve 5:

- 2 cans bouillon (beef), about 10 oz., or equiv.
- 1 cup or a little more, water
- ¼ cup dry sherry
- 2 tablespoons chopped parsley
  Salt and pepper to taste
- 1 medium avocado, peeled and diced

Heat bouillon and water, add sherry and seasonings. Cut up avocado and divide into 5 small soup bowls, and pour hot soup on top, serving at once.

Carbohydrates: Less than 2 per serving

Chicken-Clam Consommé

Suppose you have a plain dinner of hamburgers and green beans: dress it up with this light, first-course soup. Start with one can chicken broth (about 10 oz.) or equivalent, and equal amount clam broth. Just heat piping hot and serve topped with puffs of whipped cream dashed with paprika. Serve with Melba toast or rye wafers—which are the only carbohydrates in the pre-dinner course.

Mushroom Broth

For six servings, start with about ¾ lbs. fresh mushrooms, slice fine and add to 6 cups chicken broth. Simmer, covered, about 20 minutes. Strain, discarding mushrooms. At serving time, reheat adding 3 tablespoons dry sherry.

Carbohydrates: less than 3 grams per serving

Knife and Fork and Spoon Soup

Now here's the essence of 'get well': a soup that's a main course and preserves within itself the juices of all its ingredients. The following will easily serve six. It will take some preparation, but it's worth every spoonful, and is excellent reheated another day.

2   lean, meaty short ribs of beef, each cut into about 6 pieces
3   tablespoons olive oil
2   cloves garlic, minced
1   medium onion, coarsely chopped
2   quarts hot water
3   bouillon cubes or 2 teaspoons beef stock base
2   carrots, pared and cut into 1-inch pieces
2   zucchini, cut into 1-inch pieces
1   ear fresh corn, broken into 4-5 pieces
1   lb. canned, boiled onions (optional)
1   lb. small potatoes, such as fingerlings

In a deep, heavy kettle or Dutch oven heat oil and brown meat on all sides. Add garlic and onions, then hot water with bouillon cubes or beef stock base.

Simmer, covered, until beef is barely tender. Set aside to cool, then refrigerate.

Half an hour before dinner, reheat soup. Taste to see if more seasonings are needed. Add carrots and cook about 15 minutes; then put in zucchini, potatoes, and corn. Simmer about 15 minutes and add canned onions, if desired, cooking until all is thoroughly heated.

To serve, heat large soup bowls and mix a variety of all meat and vegetables into each bowl. Serve with knife, fork, and spoon, and plenty of paper napkins—the corn in this dish is finger food!

Carbohydrates: some 14 grams per serving

Wine suggestion: full-bodied red, served in tumblers

Russian Borscht

This classic is very adaptable: you can use fresh or canned beets, and add beet
juice at the end to intensify the color or dilute the bouillon. You can start with
homemade soup stock or use canned bouillon or bouillon cubes. The soup can
be served very hot, or starkly cold; it can be served with any combination of rye
bread, dill pickles, and sharp cheese.

For four servings, you'll basically need:

1   quart soup stock or bouillon
1   medium onion, chopped
3   medium raw beets, peeled, shredded
1   cup shredded cabbage
1   tablespoon lemon juice or vinegar

Simmer the onions and beets, covered, for 20-30 minutes, in the broth until
beets are tender. Add cabbage and cook another 10 minutes. Season lightly
with pepper and a touch, if any, of salt, and add lemon juice or vinegar. Serve
with spoonfuls of sour cream on each bowl. (Some cooks prefer a little more
texture by adding another shredded beet before the final heating.)

For a large party, double the recipe. Served cold, this is a way to prepare a
fine dish in advance with ease and confidence.

Carbohydrates: about 12 grams per serving

Wine suggestion: any rich red of modest pedigree

Cucumber 'Vichyssoise'

As the title indicates, this is something of a mock vichyssoise, but better than any out of a can! It can be served hot or cold, and either way it's well worth the effort.

2	cucumbers, each about 7 inches long
1	tablespoon instant minced onion
4	cups water
2	tablespoons chicken stock base
¼	teaspoon thyme
¼	teaspoon marjoram
	Pinch of oregano
1	cup light cream
1	teaspoon chopped chives or green onion

Peel cucumbers and cut up coarsely. Combine in saucepan everything except the herbs. Bring to boil, then add herbs. Simmer until cucumbers are tender, about 25 m inutes. Put through food mill, or whiz at top speed of blender. Chill thoroughly, then stir in cream. Serve very cold in small bowls with a sprinkling of chives and green onions over each. Or serve quite hot, making sure to avoid boiling so as not to curdle the cream.

Carbohydrates: about 5 grams per serving

Jellied Tomato Bouillon

Surprise! This dish you always thought is so difficult is actually easy to make, and well in advance.

1   envelope plain gelatin
¾   cup tomato juice
1   can condensed bouillon (about 10 oz.)
½   cup dry sherry
1   tablespoon lime or lemon juice
½   teaspoon Worcestershire sauce
    Lemon wedges, for serving
    Salt to taste

Soften gelatin in a little tomato juice, heating the rest with the bouillon. Add gelatin to this and stir until dissolved. Add sherry and lemon or lime juice, Worcestershire sauce, and salt as needed. Chill in refrigerator until firm. When ready to serve, stir mixture up with fork and spoon into small cups.

Carbohydrates: less than 3 grams per serving

Hot Day Soup and Salad

Soup Course: Jellied tomato bouillon, as above, with lemon slice and bread stick
Salad Course: Salmon salad platter (see p. 34)
Dessert course: Cantaloupe slice with berries or cherries, and mint garnish, served with iced coffee or tea
In a simple menu such as this, everything can be prepared in advance, ready to assemble at the last minute. Set the table with flowers and leaves to surround yourselves with summer.

Carbohydrates: 22 grams per serving

Wine suggestion: Sauvignon Blanc or Pinot Grigio

Gazpacho

Another classic that's simpler than it seems. Make sure you have ripe summer, organic tomatoes—there is no substitute in flavor. Mix with peeled diced cucumber, a little diced green pepper, diced onion, some vinegar, tomato juice, 2 tablespoons olive oil, garlic salt, dash of Tabasco, salt and pepper, and blend at high speed. Serve well chilled, garnished with lemon slices.

Carbohydrates: 10 grams in a six-ounce cup

9
NEVER NEGLECT
YOUR BEST FRIEND:
BREAD

Bread certainly has a place in a low carbohydrate diet, but don't go overboard on it! Remember, a slice of white or whole wheat or rye contains about 12 grams carbohydrate.; a roll or bun or biscuit can be almost twice as much. And that becomes about a third of your daily allotment.

One way to keep the dieter in you from feeling deprived when you have to cut back on bread is to use a little trick. Figure out various interesting ways of serving it! Instead of being tempted to eat more than you should, you will focus on the presentation and feel satisfied. Here's one simple idea: combine a little cheese or meat or other protein food with a small strip of a bread slice. The following are versions of that theme.

Peanut Butter and Tomato Sandwiches on Petite White Rounds

Allow 2 rounds of petite rye bread for each person. Spread each with 1 teaspoon peanut butter and top with a thin slice of a small tomato—in season, of course. Serve the rounds open-face, with a stalk of celery, stuffed with deviled ham, on the side.

Carbohydrates: 8 grams for each plate

Garlic-Buttered Melba Toast

Shortly before serving, spread slices of Melba toast with garlic butter, allowing 1-2 slices per person. Serve with salad for lunch or with main course for dinner. You may also break or cut each slice of toast into small pieces and add to soup or salad. Also try them with a sauce dish of heated canned tomatoes, add the pits of toast just before serving. It takes 8 slices of Melba toast, measuring 1¾ by 3½ inches, to make 1 ounce.

Carbohydrates: under 3 grams per slice

Garlic French Bread, Slim Style

Start with French or Vienna bread, thinly sliced, rather than the usual sourdough loaf, which typically is cut in thick slices or wedges, just inviting a second piece! Add enough garlic salt to soft butter to give the bread real zip. Spread slices lightly, then tie them together to recreate a loaf or portion of a loaf. Heat in 350 degree oven 10 to 15 minutes, that is, until piping hot. Allow one slice per person.

Carbohydrates: about 10 grams per slice

Krisp 'Wiches

Allow 2 rye wafers for each serving. Between them place a slice of American or cheddar cheese. Bake in 375 degree oven until thoroughly heated, about 10 minutes. These tiny sandwiches are especially good with eggs, for breakfast.

Carbohydrates: 11 grams per petite sandwich

Avocado Breakfast for Four

Scoop out and mash the pulp of half a medium avocado. Season with salt and pepper, or paprika, and 2 tablespoons lemon juice. Heap on half slices of whole wheat toast and serve with crisp bacon or fried ham.

Carbohydrates: about 7 grams per serving

Dilly Toast Sticks

Butter a slice of your favorite bread and sprinkle lightly with dill weed or dill seed. Cut into 3 sticks; arrange buttered side up on a cookie sheet and toast under low broil until browned. Allow 2-3 sticks per person.

Carbohydrates: about 4 grams per stick

Inside Out Sandwiches

Take a dilly toast stick, as above, and place on top a thin slice of ham or other ready-to-eat cold cut. Wrap meat around dilly toast and pin with cocktail pick. Try this as a pick-me-up with a green bean salad or hot buttered bean sprouts.

Carbohydrates: about 8 grams per sandwich; note that this includes even the buttered bean sprouts

Petite Rye Bread Slices

Miniature loaves of rye, designed for use as canapés, are available in most grocery or deli stores. Using these tiny slices instead of the usual size can give the illusion of abundance when several are served together. Yet four of them are about the equivalent carbohydrate count of one standard slice.

Carbohydrates: 12 grams per four petites

Toast Triangles with Hamburger and Blue Cheese

For 2 servings, cut either white or whole wheat toast diagonally to make two triangles. Top each with a thin, medium-rare ground beef patty. Crumble blue cheese over meat and slide under broiler, low, just long enough to melt cheese. Serve with garnish of tomato slice and small stalk of celery.

Carbohydrates: 7 grams per serving, including garnish

Tuna Toast Cups

Cut tops off small-to-medium size soft rolls. Fork out most of the soft doughy crumbs. Fill this cavity with a mixture of drained canned tuna, chopped pimiento, and sliced celery, well moistened with mayonnaise. Replace tops, wrap rolls in foil, and heat in 375 degree oven about 20 minutes. (Do not throw away crumbs—add to next day's meat loaf or scrambled eggs.) A mug of hot consommé goes along well with one of these toast cups.

Carbohydrates: 12-15 grams per serving

Old-Fashioned Butter Bread

This is a good way to turn day-old bread into something hot and good.

Cut slices of bread into halves crosswise. Either with a loaf pan or one improvised by folding aluminum foil to fit the bread, stand the slices with cut edges upright. Spread soft butter generously over the top edges, and bake in a very hot oven (350 degrees) for 10 or so minutes. The slices will come out with edges crisp and toasty and the centers hot and buttery.

Carbohydrates: 6 grams per each half slice

Cheese Sticks

Cut 3 bread slices into 3 sticks each. Mix 2 tablespoons melted butter (slightly cooled) into 1 beaten egg. Roll bread sticks in this mixture, then over ½ cup grated Cheddar cheese. Bake on a greased cookie sheet in moderate oven (375 degrees) until lightly browned. Serve hot. Makes 3 servings

Carbohydrates: less than 5 grams per each cheese stick

Raisin Toast Special

Cut slices of raisin bread in two. Spread lightly with soft butter, and sprinkle each even more lightly with sugar and cinnamon. Place slices on baking pan or cookie sheet and toast under low broiler 2 or 3 minutes. There are 13.3 grams carbohydrate in a slice of raisin bread, or 6.7 in a half-slice. That sprinkle of sugar costs another 2 grams. So:

Carbohydrates: about 8.7 grams carbohydrate per half slice

Skillet Grilled Cheese Sandwiches

To serve two people, spread 2 slices of your favorite bread lightly with prepared mustard, and place a slice of Cheddar cheese between them. Butter the outside of the sandwich with soft butter and brown carefully in a hot skillet, turning just as soon as first side is lightly browned. The cheese should begin to melt as soon as sandwich is turned, hence the popular name "Cheese Melts."

To serve, slice diagonally. Brown 1 or 2 Vienna sausages in the same pan and serve with sandwiches.

Carbohydrates: 12 grams per serving

About Tortillas

Freshly made or packaged tortillas are now available in most supermarkets, as Mexican cuisine has moved into the mainstream of American life. Tortillas are a pleasant alternative to bread, can substitute for most sandwiches, and often do under the common name "wraps." Good news: a 6-inch corn tortilla has a carbohydrate count of only 4.5 grams. This makes tortillas a satisfying form of bread to use frequently. They have a distinct texture as well, and store easily in the refrigerator. Like bread, they can be easily frozen, then thawed in the microwave or toaster.

To be at their best, tortillas should be served steaming hot and eaten at once. Just before serving, dampen both sides of each tortilla lightly with moistened fingers, drop onto a very hot skillet, and turn frequently until they are too hot to handle. Serve immediately in a napkin-lined basket, to be buttered and eaten as is, with soup, cheese, or favorite meat dish. But their flexibility makes them ideal for combinations with many other foods, as we will now see.

Tortilla Wraps

How about a simple frankfurter in a tortilla, one each per serving? Just brown the franks in a lightly greased skillet, heat tortillas as directed above, but with a dash of chili powder or Tabasco sauce along with the butter. Roll up the hot franks as you need them, and serve. Slice crosswise for canapés. Serve with chilled V-8 juice (not counted in carbs, below).

Carbohydrates: 10 grams per wrap

Mexican 'Sloppy Joes'

Your teenagers and picnic-loving friends will call these "cool." Here the tortillas are bite-size pieces from two well-toasted corn tortillas, to be added to ½ pound ground beef, 1 can pinto or red beans in barbecue sauce, and a tablespoon of red or green taco sauce (hot!). Cook everything in a skillet, hamburger first, and simmer until piping hot. Serve in small bowls, topped with grated Cheddar cheese. Serves four easily.

Carbohydrates: about 21 per serving

Breadstick Business

Now that packaged breadsticks come in a variety of lengths and thickness in most markets, it's a good idea to keep a package on hand to eat with salads, soups, and some main dishes. Here's the reasoning: There are about 16.5 grams carbohydrate in 1 ounce of Vienna-style breadsticks. If you buy a 5-ounce package, that's more than 82 grams. So by dividing the total number of bread-sticks into 82, you an easily figure the carb content of each stick, regardless of its size. Too complicated? Then here's a rule of thumb: the average breadstick is 5-7 grams. Be sure to store sticks tightly covered to stay crisp.

A Look at Hot Breads

If you're seriously trying to cut down on carbohydrates, you'll have to face head-on the reality of one of the most appetizing aromas on earth: the fresh from the oven aroma of hot biscuits, warming waffles, piping hot popovers, oven-filling corn bread, and warming garlic French bread. Our advice: best to cut out, and not just down!

There are times, of course, when you will bake your favorite hot bread of one kind or another to please the rest of the family or guests. If you must, the recipes for baking are all there on the packages of flour or biscuit mixes or (heavens!) cake mixes.

If you watch the rest of your carbohydrate daily diet, you can have that occasional baking treat. But there's little reason for this book to offer you those recipes.

10
DESSERTS
HAVE A PLACE ON
YOUR TABLE

Is it possible to have dessert on the Drinking Man's Diet? Yes, indeed. Perhaps not every day, but frequently enough. Here are some strategies for restraint:

Instead of eating fruit for breakfast or lunch, occasionally turn it into dessert for dinner. For example, 3 or 4 slices of a tart apple with a slice of cheese. Or combine a low-carbohydrate sweet with an after-dinner drink—perhaps a Lorna Doone cookie with a glass of hot-buttered rum, just right for a cold winter's night. That cookie packs only 5.4 grams of carbs, and the rum none.

Cut down, too, on serving sizes. According to the Tables at the back of this book, a slice of pound cake contains 14.8 grams carbohydrate. Cut that slice into quarters, and you have 3.7 grams per piece. When you set out a plate with a number of these quarter slices, few people, including you, will take more than 1 or 2 to go with after-dinner coffee or that last cup of tea.

Check up, too, on your serving dishes. Often a small serving of dessert is more effective in just the right size dish or cup than a larger serving. Consider: one-third of a cup of custard in a dessert dish looks skimpy, but in a small roly-poly glass it looks interesting. Good restaurants know this trick!

Watermelon Balls in Champagne

With a sharp, small spoon, scoop melon balls from a slice of seeded watermelon. Arrange 3 balls in bottom of each champagne glass, and set to chill. Near the end of the main dinner course, pour pink champagne over the melon balls and bring to table immediately. Guests sip the champagne and then enjoy the well-flavored melon as dessert.

Carbohydrates: about 6 grams per serving

Cantaloupe Slices with Berries or Cherries

You can usually get 5 or 6 crosswise slices out of a cantaloupe weighing about a pound—enough for 4 servings. Save the end pieces left over for next day's breakfast or lunch. Slice the melon, scoop out seeds, and pare each slice. Chill until dessert time, then arrange on individual dessert plates. Fill centers with ½ cup sliced strawberries or a few ripe cherries. Garnish with mint if you have some on hand.

Carbohydrates: about 9 grams per average serving

Sherried Pear Halves

An hour or more before serving time, pour dry sherry over dietetic canned pear halves and add 2-3 strips of lemon peel. Cover and chill. When it's time for dessert, take up sherried pears into small shallow dishes, half a pear for each serving. Dash with nutmeg and provide a small pitcher of additional sherry for those who wish it.

Carbohydrates: 9 grams per serving from fruit, another 3-4 from sherry

Grape Extravaganza

When grapes are at their best, in the fall, make the most of them. For a small dinner party, for example, you can feature grapes in the centerpiece, on the vine. At dessert time, bring on small plates each containing a small 'bunchlet' of grapes, plus a spoonful or so of Roquefort or equivalent cheese dip. Provide scissors for those who wish to clip more grapes from the centerpiece, for the dip.

Carbohydrates: about 15 grams for a bunch of about a dozen grapes, including the cheese dip

Wine suggestion: Grenache Rose or any of the cross-over reds, such as white Zinfandel or white Shiraz.

Zabaglione

Every chef or good cook has his or her own way of making this classic Italian dessert. Some insist that a true Zabaglione is made just before serving and uses only the yolks of the eggs. Others prefer whole eggs and make the dessert well in advance; then, as it is removed from the refrigerator and is still cool, they fold in stiffly whipped cream, and chill again before serving.

All agree that zabaglione should be served in stemmed wine glasses or old-fashioned sherbet cups.

The following recipe is something of a compromise. To serve six, take 6 eggs, 4 tablespoons confectioner's powdered sugar, and a dash of salt, mix and heat in the top of a double boiler. Beat constantly with a portable mixer or manual rotary beater for about 8 minutes. As you do, also beat in 6 tablespoons dry sherry or white wine. Mixture should stiffen, enough to hold a small spoon upright in the center. Now pour the mixture into chilled wine glasses, if to be served cold, or in warm cups if preferred hot. It will hold up better, of course, if chilled.

Carbohydrates: 8-10 grams per serving

Walnut Bars

If you're cooking for a family, it's fun to make cookies for all to enjoy – even though you or another family member may be watching the carbohydrates. Store-bought cookies are inevitably disastrous for a diet. But some recipes you can follow at home spare a lot of the carbohydrates. Here's one good one:

- 1 **cup light brown sugar, firmly packed**
- 1 **egg unbeaten**
- 1 **teaspoon vanilla**
- ½ **cup all-purpose flour**
- ¼ **teaspoon each, soda and salt**
- 1 **cup coarsely chopped walnuts**

Stir sugar, egg and vanilla together in a bowl (don't beat hard). Sift flour with soda and salt and stir in; add nuts. Spread this stiff batter into 8" square greased shallow pan. Bake at 350 degrees for 20 minutes, until browned but still soft. (Top will puff up while baking, then sink.) Remove from oven but let cool in pan until just warm enough to cut into 1½ inch squares. Makes about 25 "brownies." (Chocolate brownies will have raisins and dark chocolate.)

Carbohydrates: about 7 grams per bar

Custard Sauce for Fruit

Yes, a custard—soft type or baked—does contain a good many grams of carbohydrate. But the eggs and milk in it make it useful in a well-rounded diet. These are basic directions for a soft custard:

- 2 **cups milk**
- 2 **eggs or 4 yolks**
- ¼ **cup sugar, or an artificial sweetener**
  Dash of salt
- ½ **teaspoon vanilla**
- ½ **teaspoon lemon extract**

1 or 2 drops almond extract, optional

Scald most of the milk in top of double boiler. Beat eggs lightly with remaining cold milk, sweetener, and salt (the cold milk keeps the egg from forming lumps with the sugar or sweetener). Add this mixture slowly into warm milk, and cook, stirring constantly about 5 minutes. Test frequently by dipping a clean spoon into the mixture – when the spoon begins to coat, remove top from double boiler and pour custard through a fine strainer. Add flavorings and cool.

Cover custard and store in back area of refrigerator. The result should be a little over a pint, serving six or more. Try custard on dietetic canned fruits as well as serving solo.

Carbohydrates: about 1½ grams per tablespoon

Whipped Gelatin with Whipped Topping

Four servings will result from a 3-oz. package of fruit-flavored gelatin. To make it serve six, pour the congealed gelatin into a bowl and whip with a fork until well broken up. Serve in small dishes or wine stems, with topping of whipped cream. For the latter you may also substitute whipped cream cheese or even a non-dairy topping, readily available in supermarkets.

The low-fat topping in the following recipe is another alternative.

Carbohydrates: 12-14 grams per serving, depending on the topping

Low Fat Whipped Topping

If you're conscious of too many fats in your diet, consider this alternative to whipped cream. Some desserts just cry out for whipped cream as a finishing touch, and this one will satisfy that need.

For 2 cups, enough for 16 servings, you can see the only culprit is really the sugar. You can also halve the recipe if it's not likely you will be serving it again soon.

½   **cup nonfat dry milk**
½   **cup cold water**
1   **tablespoon sugar**
½   **cup vanilla**
1   **tablespoon lemon juice**

Sprinkle nonfat dry milk over water in a bowl. Beat at high speed, until thick. Gradually beat in sugar, then vanilla and lemon juice, continuing to beat until stiff enough to hold soft peaks. Simple enough?

Carbohydrates: With a total of 33, only about 2 grams per serving

About Sugar

Since a tablespoon of powdered sugar contains only 8 grams carbohydrate as opposed to 12 grams in granulated sugar, it's a good idea to substitute powdered to sprinkle over fruits or other desserts. There are also frosting sugars, very light in weight, that have even fewer grams per spoonful—and these seem just as sweet when poured over desserts. Consider using them to keep that count down!

Postscript

If you really crave an after-dinner sweet, try any one of many low-calorie gelatin desserts now on the market. Artificial sweeteners have come a long way. But study the labels and avoid anything with a lot of corn syrup – this is the unfortunate result of national food policy that concentrated on removing fat from foods and so opened the door to corn syrup.

Dessert should be an occasional pleasure, not an exercise in chemistry. Keep your focus on that magic number: 60 grams a day of carbohydrates. Remember, too few can be as undesirable as too many.

11
A DAY AT A TIME

Breakfast, lunch, and dinner constitute the way most of us eat our way through life. And that's how it should be. With minor exceptions, it's better to eat three (some would say more) times a day rather than skip breakfast, in the rush to get to work or school, and then gorge at night while watching Monday Night Football or the latest sitcom.

Food eaten after four o'clock in the afternoon, without further exercise for the day, is more likely to "go to fat" than food eaten in the morning, and worked off during our most active hours. This is common sense.

So in this chapter, we're focusing on menus that work for each of the normal "three squares." Let's review what the experts tell us about these choices. The U.S. Department of Agriculture, whose tables we use for carbohydrate counting, began recommending that we pay attention to the "4 Basic Food Groups." Thus we had:

Milk Group: All dairy products, including cheese and ice cream. Children and teenagers should eat about twice what adults need, the latter only about two cups a day. But how much of a cup is a slice of Gorgonzola?

Meat Group: Two or more servings of meat, poultry, fish, eggs, and alternatives in dry beans, peas, nuts. Meats are peas?

Vegetables and fruits: Four or more servings a day or dark greens, yellows, reds—such as peppers and tomatoes, and all sorts of fruits. This opened the marketing campaign for orange juice and corn, each becoming sweeter by the day.

Bread and Cereal Group: Four or more servings of grains. Unfortunately, little distinction was made between white bread and whole grains. It took years for this loophole to be closed. Notice how the last two food groups contain most of the carbohydrates.

Then along came the "Food Pyramid." Greater emphasis was placed on the "good" carbohydrates in green, leafy vegetables and unsugary fruit. We were now supposed to get six servings of these a day.

The Drinking Man's Diet, bursting on the scene in 1964, correctly singled out the sugars and starches among the "food groups" as the enemy of a good weight-control plan. Others pounced on the idea without noticing that this diet *requires* about 60 grams of carbohydrates a day. In their zeal to shed weight, people came to believe, as the faddists told them, that less is always better!

There are several low-carbohydrate diets that to this day ignore the need for balance among carbohydrates. You just can't eat all the rich steaks and sauces in the effort to lower your carbohydrates. Excessive fat in the diet matters. Insufficient carbohydrate in the diet matters.

What it comes down to is, you must have balance. In this chapter we'll see how meals can be easily balanced throughout the day. We'll do this with full-day menus!

Through the Day Menus

You don't have to follow the following menus literally. They're here to give you ideas. Ideas about variety among those 60 grams. Ideas about stretching foods to thin out the carbohydrates. Ideas about meal planning.

If this diet is for your own weight control or weight loss, and no one else in your family, the carbohydrate amounts are simple to follow. If you're cooking for children, simply allow for extra servings of the carbohydrates for them. There's been much publicity recently about obesity among children; but this is not our focus. There are so many causes for childhood obesity that a physician's advice must come first.

As the title of this book clearly implies, we assume you have drinks with some regularity. As the Tables in the back of this book clearly show, there are few carbohydrates in most alcoholic beverages, save beer and sweet wine. A popular misconception is that alcohol contains sugar and/or converts to sugar and therefore must contribute to excessive carbohydrates. This is plainly wrong —unless you choose to ignore the Department of Agriculture and the FDA.

Taking off weight by means of carbohydrate counting has been successful for millions of people. Unlike highly restrictive diets, this one allows you to enjoy a very wide variety of foods. In fact, no specific foods are restricted in this diet! Certain high-carbohydrate foods are simply kept within bounds. So read the following pages with this in mind. Here are two weeks' worth of daily menus, not one of which exceeds 60 grams a day!

1

Breakfast Creamed chipped beef (1 cup) on half slice of toast. Coffee or tea. (18 grams)

Easy-to-pack lunch 2 skillet-browned frankfurters with a teaspoon of prepared mustard. Half slice buttered bread. Tea, coffee, or diet cold drink. (9 grams)

Dinner in Half an Hour Chicken Paprika (see p. 55). 5 pieces French-fried potatoes (frozen, reheated). 1 cup green bean salad with 1 or 2 sliced fresh mushrooms added. (See salads, p. 96) Dessert cup of ½ grapefruit cut into bite-sized pieces and topped with whipped cream cheese (28 grams)

Total carbohydrate for the day: 55 grams

2

Quick to fix breakfast 3 tablespoons canned corned beef hash, lightly browned, topped with poached egg. Coffee (7 grams)

Pack and carry lunch Peanut butter and lettuce sandwich on 1 slice b read. Generous slice of Swiss cheese. Stalk of celery and six olives (16 grams)

Dinner Big serving of baked canned ham. ½ cup mashed winter squash. ½ cup herb seasoned canned shoestring beets. Apple celery, and walnut salad on lettuce, with favorite dressing: ½ small apple, diced, 1 stalk celery, sliced, 4 walnuts, chopped coarsely. (33 grams)

Total carbohydrates for the day: 56 grams

3

Breakfast Cheese-scrambled eggs (See p. 66). Half slice toast. Coffee. (12 grams)

Take it with you lunch 1 3-oz. can chicken, opened and sprinkled with seasoned salt or dill salt. Slice of Melba toast. 8-oz carton of milk, if available. (18 grams)

Dinner in a hurry King-size hamburgers with garnish of 5 corn chips and 2-3 slices tomato on lettuce. 1 cup broccoli spears with 3 tablespoons Mock Hollandaise sauce (see p. 94). Half slice bread. (24 grams)

Total carbohydrates for the day: 54 grams

4

Breakfast ½ cup cottage cheese with ¼ of a banana, sliced. Rye wafer. Coffee (14 grams)

Lunch When cooking hamburgers the evening before, cook an extra one. Then, for this lunch-time sandwich, crumble meat, mix with mayonnaise and spread between 2 half slices bread. Add 2-3 slices dill pickle. (15 grams)

Dinner Broiled salmon filets. Halves of small potatoes, precooked, then broiled along with salmon. 1 cup canned zucchini (or fresh, cooked) in tomato sauce. Lettuce salad, mayonnaise with 2 slices crumbled bacon. (28 grams)

Total carbohydrates for the day: 57 grams

5

Breakfast 1 cup tomato juice over ice. 1-2 fried eggs. Half slice toast. Coffee (16 grams)

Quick Lunch at Lunch Counter 1 cup clam chowder or chicken soup. 2 saltines. Have a slice of cheese from home for afternoon snack. (18 grams)

Dinner 2-oz. serving of fried liver with 4 slices crisp-cooked bacon. Half small potato, chopped and fried in bacon fat from above. Cottage cheese bowl with shredded lettuce (see p. 100). Red wine. (20 grams)

Total carbohydrates for the day: 54 grams

6

Breakfast 3-4 canned meatballs, cocktail type, browned in butter. Half a donut, split crosswise. Coffee. (9 grams)

Lunch Away or at Home Swiss cheese sandwich on slice of mustard buttered rye bread. ½ cup milk. (18 grams)

Dinner Meaty pork chop, glazed carrot (see p. 86). Frozen spinach (1 cup), buttered. Half a small grapefruit, broiled. Small sugary cookie, such as walnut square (see p. 126). Incidentally, it takes just a few minutes to mix and bake them. (33 grams)

Total carbohydrates for the day: 60 grams

7

Breakfast Milk toast—1 slice toast with ¾ cups hot milk. Coffee. (21 grams)
Lunch 2 slices canned corned beef, on half slice rye bread. 2-3 stuffed olives.
2 apple wedges. (12 grams)
Dinner Mug of hot consommé; 2-3 pieces celery. 2 slices roast turkey roll. ½
cup buttered noodles with sesame seeds added. Generous seafood salad—shredded lettuce with canned crabmeat or shrimp, Thousand Island dressing. Glass
of dry sherry for dessert. Follow directions on package of frozen turkey roll.
Have noodles piping hot. (23 grams)

Total carbohydrates for the day: 56 grams

8

Breakfast Scrambled eggs with little sausages. Half slice toast. Coffee.
(7 grams)
Lunch ¾ cup cottage cheese with ½ fresh peach. 2 crackers, 10 salted
almonds. (18 grams)
Dinner Instant appetizer salad—celery, olives, and 3-4 salami slices. Baked
veal chop (see p. 45). Five canned artichoke hearts, sliced and seasoned with
herb salt. Half slice Vienna bread. ½ cup milk, later, for a 'night cap'.
(26 grams)

Total carbohydrates for the day: 51 grams

9

Breakfast Treat 1 small pancake. 2 slices Canadian bacon. 1 teaspoon jam or
jelly. Coffee. (13 grams)
Leisurely Lunch Crunchy Tuna Salad (see p. 102). Bread stick. ½ cup milk.
(20 grams)
Dinner Large serving of pot roast (see p. 32). Half slice bread. 1 cup diced
turnips or ½ cup diced rutabagas. 1 cup shredded carrot-and-cabbage salad in
lettuce cup, with favorite salad dressing. (26 grams)

Total carbohydrates for the day: 59 grams

10

Semi-continental Breakfast Thin slice of peeled cantaloupe. Fried ham. Half a soft roll. Café au lait—½ cup hot milk with ½ cup coffee. (18 grams)
Lunch Half slice toast with ¼ cup cheddar cheese sauce (see p. 63) Deviled egg, wrapped in lettuce for eating from hand. Hot tea. (11 grams)
Dinner 1½ slices special meat loaf (see p. 38). ½ ear corn, fresh or frozen, cooked. 1 cup cauliflower seasoned with butter and ¼ cup milk. 3 slices fresh cucumber or dill pickle. Tea or coffee. As meat loaf takes more than an hour to mix and bake, it can be made the day before and served cold with hot vegetables. (29 grams)

Total carbohydrates for the day: 58

11

Breakfast Omelet with Spanish sauce (see p. 68), or simply scrambled eggs with the sauce. Half slice of toast. Coffee. (12 grams)
Lunch Open face hamburger on half toasted hamburger bun. 1 teaspoon catsup. Half cup milk. (18 grams)
Special Dinner Generous serving of roast leg of lamb (use fresh herbs and garlic, roast to degree of doneness preferred by you, usually about 1½ hours in very hot oven). 1 cup buttered chard—cooked from fresh or frozen. 3 small roasted potatoes, browned with roast. Parsley garnish. 2 slices tomato, topped with 1 teaspoon chopped green pepper, French dressing.

Total carbohydrate for the day: 60 grams

12

Breakfast Half cup orange juice over ice. Hard cooked egg, sprinkled with seasoning salt. Rye wafer. Coffee. (18 grams)
Early lunch Half slice bread spread thickly with deviled ham. Half cup milk. (12 grams)
Dinner Generous serving pounded round steak, fried in oil and butter. Red cabbage with wine (see p. 85). 1 cup Green Beans Almondine (see p. 79). 5 large strawberries with spoonful of whipped cream cheese for dipping. Tea or coffee. (30 grams)

Total carbohydrates for the day: 60 grams

13

Breakfast Shirred egg in canned stewed tomato (see p. 69). Rye wafer. Coffee. (7 grams)

Paper-Bag Lunch One 3-oz can tuna, opened and drained before packing lunch, and sprinkled with dill weed. 5 potato chips. 2 raw carrot sticks. (7 grams)

Chicken Dinner Mug of hot canned chicken broth to sip while dinner is cooking. 1 large or 2 smaller pieces of broiled chicken, breasts or thighs. ¾ cup creamed peas (fresh or frozen). Sauerkraut salad (½ cup kraut, drained, and mixed with mayonnaise). Serve in lettuce cup and garnish with slice of canned pimiento. Pound cake, 1 slice, or whipped gelatin with whipped cream or other topping see p. 127). (42 grams)

Total carbohydrate for the day: 58 grams

14

Breakfast Small ground beef patty, with half slice toast. 1 teaspoon jelly or jam, or half of a peeled and sectioned tangerine. Coffee. (11 grams)

Lunch 1 cup oyster stew. 2 saltines. Cheddar cheese wedge. (18 grams)

Dinner 2 broiled lamb chops, 1 slice eggplant, broiled. 2 fresh mushrooms, broiled. 1 cup Italian beans, fresh cooked or frozen. 6 spears canned asparagus on lettuce with garnish of 3 thin slices of red-skinned apple for color and texture, amounting to about ¼ apple. Roquefort or equivalent dressing. Half slice favorite bread. Tea or coffee. (27 grams)

Total carbohydrates for the day: 56 grams

Daily Wine Choices

In the preceding two-week schedule of breakfasts, lunches, and dinners coming close to 60 grams of carbohydrates per day, no mention was made of wine selections. But wine is clearly a logical accompaniment for dinner, as is the pre-dinner beverage of your choice. Here are some general considerations, rather than specific wines for certain main courses:

1.   **"Drink what you like," you hear, but don't believe it.** Educate your taste by reading the wine column in your local paper, trading ideas with friends, and experimenting. Most people tend to sweeter wines, perhaps because sweetness is built in to our food culture. Tartness may turn one off at first, but it's a natural with most foods. This is why lemon enhances most vegetables and fish, and vinegar brings out flavors in stews.

2.   **White with fish, red with meat.** Yes indeed, but it's more a matter of balance than color. There are some strong whites (big Chardonnays, for example), and there are delicate reds (old-fashioned Zinfandels, many Pinot Noirs). Again, experiment.

3.   **Home in on your favorites.** Establish benchmarks of wines that you know you like. Venture forth from there. Always have a "house red" or "house white" in your home that you know you can trust.

12
SPECIAL CASES, SPECIAL PACES

We said this at the beginning, and we'll repeat it here: this is a diet for normally healthy people. Be fore-warned: if you're trying to lose a very large amount of weight—that is, approaching 10 percent of your body weight—you must have your doctor's approval of any diet plan. Any plan.

If you're about 200 pounds and want to lose 20 pounds, by all means see you doctor first. If you want to lose 10 pounds or so, you probably are not going to stress your system enough to need professional advice.

This book in no way offers medical advice. Everyone's physical condition is unique. If, in addition to being overweight, you have heart conditions, diabetes, or any other physical problem, do not undertake any dietary plan without professional advice.

But there is some encouraging news about the Drinking Man's Diet that puts it in a class above the fads that have come and gone over the last forty years. The largest HMO in the country now routinely advises its members to cut down on the carbohydrates that are the worst offenders: white bread, pasta, white rice, potatoes, and anything with large amounts of sugar. Why? Because those foods provide extremely large amounts of calories without proportionate amounts of nutrients.

We're not even talking here about soft drinks, which are now properly termed "liquid corn" because of the corn syrup that is their main ingredient.

The Chronic Diseases and Weight

Medical theory seems to waver back and forth on this topic, but in general it's agreed that being overweight is a risk factor in all the chronic diseases. You can lower your blood pressure with less stress and less weight o carry around. You can counter strong genetic tendencies to diabetes with proper weight control. You can get better nutrition in general if your appetite for good foods isn't overwhelmed by your devotion to "empty calories."

And then there's this: when you move your belt size to new points, when you find you can button your shirts more easily, when you have less trouble bending over to tie your shoes, you're a different person! You're more confident of your abilities. You've actually accomplished something few people can claim to have done: you've lost weight and kept off weight!

Isn't that frame of mind worth a lot?

Eating Better and Moving Better

You will discover, after you've been on this diet for a reasonable length of time, that you're learning important things about food values. And you'll subtly learn something else: food cannot be separated from your general lifestyle.

Exercise is no longer an option for the dietary conscious person. You absolutely must "move" more to gain the full benefits of this or any other diet. You cannot be a "couch potato" and pretend to make up for a sedentary lifestyle with dietary "fixes."

You must breathe in and out in a different way once you take better control over your body. You will find yourself walking up stairs when once you waited for the escalator or elevator. You will walk to a store five blocks away instead of getting into your car automatically. You will not do these things because you have joined a fitness club or bought a home exercise device, but because you just *can* walk that extra distance without puffing and you *can* pull your socks on without getting red in the face. The changes come oh so gradually, but then they build on each other.

Make those changes work for your diet and work for all your moving parts. Exercise is not about running marathons. It's about running your life.

Now, About Those Breadsticks...

In the previous chapter, where a full two weeks of 60-grams-per-day menus are laid out in detail, you've seen a lot about a half slice of bread, a strip of celery, five olives, and three grapefruit sections. Sounds like the usual abstention diet, doesn't it?

Think again. Once you become accustomed to limiting the usual carbohydrate sources, you'll gravitate easily to smaller portions, in which you actually count things that go in your mouth and hold back on seconds of cookies and the usual croissant with the morning coffee. You might well ask, Do I really want to give up that scone with dried cranberries, that chocolate-raisin brownie with a glass of Port, that Ben and Jerry's Chunky Monkey?

It's your choice. But little by little it will become an obvious choice. In social situations, you will want to say "I'll go along with the crowd." More and more these days, as people around you decline desserts for no obvious reason, you'll not feel like the "person on a diet" but more like the person who just likes something else better.

It isn't between a breadstick and an almond torte. It's between what you want for your body and what you thoughtlessly used to want for the taste of sugar.

The best motivation, in that event, will come from changes that you can observe, really in just a short time, in your own weight and belt size. Use the food values expressed throughout this book, and in fine detail in the Tables that follow, to change your mindset about what's good for you to eat.

We hope this Cookbook is a positive step forward toward making good food choices for yourself and for those for whom you cook.

TABLE OF CARBOHYDRATES GRAMS CONTENT OF FOOD

	MEASUREMENT	GRAMS OF CARBOHYDRATE
MILK, CREAM, CHEESE; RELATED PRODUCTS		
Milk: Cow's	1 cup	12
Nonfat	1 cup	12
Buttermilk	1 cup	12
Evaporated	1 cup	29
Condensed	1 cup	170
Dry, whole	1 cup	39
Dry, nonfat	1 cup	42
Soy	1 cup	4
Milk: Goat's	1 cup	11
Cream		
Half-n-Half	1 cup	11
	1 tablespoon	1
Light, table	1 cup	10
or coffee	1 tablespoon	1
Whipping Medium	1 cup	8
	1 tablespoon	1
Heavy	1 cup	7
	1 tablespoon	trace
Sour cream, low-fat	1 tablespoon	1
Yogurt, plain whole milk	8 ounces	11
Plain low fat	8 ounces	16
Yogurt w/fruit, low fat	8 ounces	43
Cheese		
Blue, Roquefort	1 ounce	trace
Cheddar or American	1 ounce	trace
Cottage cheese, non-fat	1 cup	6
Mozzarella	1 ounce	1
Monterey jack	1 ounce	1
Swiss	1 ounce	1
Provolone	1 ounce	1
Parmesan	1 tablespoon	trace
Ricotta	1 cup	8
Tofu	block	2
EGGS		
White, raw fresh	1 large	trace
Yolk, raw fresh	1 large	trace
Hard boiled	1 large	1
Poached	1 large	1
Scrambled	1 large	1
MEAT		
Beef		
Sirloin	3 ounces	0
Cold cuts	2 ounces	1
Ground	3 ounces	0
Heart	3 ounces	1
Hot dog	3 ounces	0

	MEASUREMENT	GRAMS OF CARBOHYDRATE
Jerky	1 ounce	0
Kidney	3 ounces	1
Liver	2 ounces	6
Rib roast	3 ounces	0
Round	3 ounces	0
Stew meat	3 ounces	0
Sweetbreads	1 serving	0
Tongue	3 ounces	trace
Veal	3 ounces	0
Lamb		
Leg of lamb	3 ounces	0
Chop	4 ounces	0
Shoulder	3 ounces	0
Kidney	3 oz	1
liver	3 oz	3
Pork		
Fresh ham	3 oz	0
loin chops	3 oz	0
Loin roast	3 oz	0
shoulder	3 oz	0
back ribs	3 oz	0
Cured ham	3 oz	0
Cured bacon	3 slices	1
Canadian grilled	2 slices	trace
Sausage	2 links	trace
FISH		
Mackerel	1 serving	0
Butterfish	1 serving	0
Eel, smoked	1 serving	0
Flounder	1 serving	0
Salmon	1 serving	0
Smoked	3 ounces	0
Shad	1 serving	0
Sole	1 serving	0
Frogs legs	1 serving	0
Haddock, smoked	1 serving	0
Halibut	1 serving	0
Sword fish	1 serving	0
Herring	1 serving	0
Perch	1 serving	0
Pompano	1 serving	0
Sturgeon	1 serving	0
Tuna	1 serving	0
Scallop	3 ounces	3
Whitefish	1 serving	0
Trout	1 serving	0
Anchovies	1 serving	trace
Lobster	1 serving	trace

	MEASUREMENT	GRAMS OF CARBOHYDRATE
Shad roe	1 serving	trace
Shrimp	3 ounces	1
Crab meat	3 ounces	1
Sardines	3 ounces	1
Clams	3 ounces	4
Abalone	3 ounces	3
Bass		
Orange roughy	3 ounces	0
Oysters, raw	1 cup	8
Fish sticks	8 ounces	15

POULTRY & GAME

	MEASUREMENT	GRAMS OF CARBOHYDRATE
Chicken		
Boneless breast	1 large	0
Leg w/ bone	4 ounces	0
Liver	1 liver	trace
Thigh	1 small	0
Giblets	1 cup	2
Duck		
Domesticated	½ lb.	0
Goose	½ lb.	0
Turkey	½lb.	0
Giblets	1 cup	3
Quail	½ lb.	0
Pheasant	½ lb.	0
Capon	½ lb.	0
Rabbit	½ lb.	0
Venison	½ lb.	0

VEGETABLES

	MEASUREMENT	GRAMS OF CARBOHYDRATE
Artichoke cooked, boiled, drained	1 cup	19
Asparagus cooked, boiled drained	4 spears	3
Bamboo shoots, canned	1 cup	4
Beans all cooked, boiled without salt		
Baked	1 cup	52
Bean sprouts	1 cup	4
Black	1 cup	41
Garbanzo	1 cup	45
Kidney	1 cup	40
Lentils	1 cup	40
Lima	1 cup	29
Mung	1 cup	6
Navy	1 cup	48
Pinto	1 cup	43
Refried, canned	1 cup	39
Snap green	1 cup	10
Soy bean	1 cup	20
White	1 cup	57
Beets, cooked, boiled	1 cup	17
Canned	1 beet	2
Greens	1cup	8
Broccoli, cooked, boiled	1 cup	8
raw	1 cup	5
frozen	1 cup	10
Brussels sprouts	1 cup	13
frozen	1 cup	13
Cabbage , cooked, boiled	1 cup	7
red, raw	1 cup	4
Chinese	1 cup	3
Carrots, cooked, boiled	1 cup	16
canned	1 cup	8
frozen	1 cup	12
raw	1 cup	11
Cauliflower		
cooked, boiled	1 cup	5
frozen	1 cup	7
raw	1 cup	5
Celery, cooked boiled	1 cup	6
raw	1 cup	4
Collards, cooked, boiled	1 cup	9
frozen	1 cup	12
Corn, sweet, cooked ,boiled		
white/ yellow	1 ear	19
Frozen	1 cup	32
Creamed	1 cup	46
Cucumber, raw	1 cup	3
Eggplant, cooked, boiled	1 cup	7
Endive, raw	1 cup	2
Kale, cooked, boiled	1 cup	7
Frozen	1 cup	7
Leeks, cooked, boiled	1 cup	8
Lettuce		
Iceberg	1 cup	1
Butter	1 cup	1
Romaine	1 cup	1
Loose leaf	1 cup	2
Mushrooms,		
cooked, boiled	1 cup	8
raw	1 cup	3
shiitake	1 cup	21
Mustard greens,		
cooked, boiled	1 cup	3
Okra, cooked, boiled	1 cup	12
frozen	1 cup	11
Onions, cooked, boiled	1 cup	21
raw	1 cup	14
Parsley	10 sprigs	trace
Parsnips, cooked, boiled	1 cup	30
Peas, green fresh	1 cup	19
frozen	1 cup	23
Canned	1 cup	21

	MEASUREMENT	GRAMS OF CARBOHYDRATE		MEASUREMENT	GRAMS OF CARBOHYDRATE
Peppers, sweet, raw			Avocado, California	½ avocado	6
green / red	1 cup	10	Florida	½ avocado	11
hot Chile	1 pepper	4	Banana, raw	1	28
Jalapeno, canned	¼ cup	1	Blackberries	1 cup	18
Potatoes			Blueberries	1 cup	20
boiled, cooked in skin	1 potato	27	Frozen, sweetened	1 cup	50
without skin		27	Cantaloupe	1 cup	13
without skin, baked		33	Cherries, raw, sweet	10 cherries	11
with skin, baked		43	Canned	1 cup	22
mashed with whole milk, 1 cup		37	Cranberry sauce, canned	1 cup	142
French fried, frozen,			Dates, dried	1 cup	131
home prepared in oven	10 fries	15	Figs	1 fig	12
Scalloped with butter	1 cup	26	Grapes, seedless	1 cup	28
Sweet,			Grapefruit	½ grapefruit	10
cooked, baked in skin	1 potato	35	Canned	1 cup	39
without skin		38	Honeydew	1 cup	16
canned	1 cup	54	Kiwi	1 medium	11
Radish, raw	1 radish	trace	Lemon	1 lemon	5
Rutabagas, cooked, boiled	1 cup	15	Mandarin orange	1 orange	9
Sauerkraut, canned	1 cup	10	Mangos	1 cup	28
Seaweed, raw, kelp	2 tbsp.	trace	Nectarine	1 nectarine	16
Spinach, cooked, boiled	1 cup	7	Oranges	1 cup	21
frozen	1 cup	10	Papaya	1 cup	14
raw	1 cup	1	Peach	1 cup	19
Squash, all varieties			canned in syrup	1 cup	52
cooked, boiled	1 cup	8	Pear	1 pear	25
baked	1 cup	18	canned in syrup	1 cup	51
Turnips, cooked, boiled	1 cup	8	Pineapple	1 cup	19
			canned in syrup	1 cup	51
HERBS			Plum	1 plum	9
All spice	1 tsp.	1	canned in syrup	1 cup	60
Basil	1 tsp.	trace	Prunes, dried,		
Caraway	1 tsp.	1	stewed without sugar	1 cup	70
Celery salt	1 tsp.	trace	dried, uncooked	5 prunes	26
Cinnamon	1 tsp.	2	Raisins	1 cup	148
Chives	1 tsp.	0	Raspberries	1 cup	14
Coriander	1 tsp.	trace	Rhubarb, frozen		
Dill	1 tsp.	1	with sugar	1 cup	75
Garlic	1 clove	trace	Strawberries	1 cup	12
Saffron	1 tsp.	trace	Frozen	1 cup	66
Salt	1 tsp.	0	Tangerine	1 tangerine	9
Thyme	1 tsp.	trace	Tomatillo	1 medium	2
			Tomato	1 tomato	6
FRUITS AND FRUIT PRODUCTS			cherry	1 cherry tomato	2
Apple	1 raw	21	canned, stewed	1 cup	17
Applesauce			canned, whole	1 cup	10
sweetened	1 cup	51	puree	1 cup	23
unsweetened	1 cup	28	paste	1 cup	51
dried	1 rings	21	sun-dried	1 piece	1
Apricots	1 raw	4	sun-dried in oil	1 piece	trace
dried	10 halves	22	Watermelon	1 cup	11
canned in syrup	1 cup	55			

	MEASUREMENT	GRAMS OF CARBOHYDRATE
BREADS AND GRAIN PRODUCTS		
Bagel, 4" bagel		
cinnamon raisin	1 bagel	39
Plain, onion, garlic,		
poppy seed, sesame		48
Biscuit	1 biscuit	45
Breads		
Banana	1 slice	33
corn	1 slice	28
cracked wheat	1 slice	12
Croissant	1	26
Croutons	1 cup	25
French, sourdough	1 slice	26
Italian	1 slice	10
multi grain	1 slice	12
oatmeal	1 slice	13
pita	1 pocket	33
Pumpernickel	1 slice	15
raisin	1 slice	13
Rye	1 slice	15
reduced calorie	1 slice	9
White	1 slice	12
reduced calorie	1 slice	10
wheat	1 slice	11
reduced calorie	1 slice	10
whole wheat	1 slice	13
Breadcrumbs,		
grated, seasoned	1 cup	84
Bread stuffing	1 cup	43
Barley, pearled, raw	1 cup	155
cooked	1 cup	44
Bulgur, dry	1 cup	106
Cooked	1 cup	34
Buckwheat flour	1 cup	85
Cooked	1 cup	34
Carob flour	1 tbsp	7
Cornmeal, yellow	1 cup	94
Couscous, dry	1 cup	134
cooked	1 cup	36
Crackers		
Saltines	4 crackers	9
rye, wafers, plain	1 wafer	9
Melba toast	4 pieces	15
Graham	4 crackers	10
Noodles, egg	1 cup	40
Pancakes		
plain, frozen		
(includes buttermilk)	1 pancake	15
plain, dry mix	1 pancake	14
Pasta		
enriched	1 cup	37
un-enriched	1 cup	37

	MEASUREMENT	GRAMS OF CARBOHYDRATE
Oatmeal	1 cup	26
Rice		
brown, long grain,		
cooked	1 cup	45
white, long grain,		
cooked	1 cup	45
Seeds		
sunflower, dry	1 ounce	7
sesame, dry	1 tbsp	trace
pumpkin	1 ounce	4
Waffles, frozen	1 waffle	13
Wheat flour, white,		
all purpose, enriched	1 cup	95
Wheat flour, whole grain	1 cup	87
Wild rice, cooked	1 cup	35
CEREALS		
Cheerios, regular	1 cup	22
apple cinnamon	1 cup	31
Honey nut	1 cup	24
Corn flakes	1 cup	17
Golden Grahams	1 cup	30
Raisin bran	1 cup	48
Total	1 cup	28
Wheat bran	1 cup	34
Wheaties	1 cup	24
Froot Loops	1 cup	26
Frosted Flakes	1 cup	35
Rice Crispies	1 cup	22
Granola, with raisins	1 cup	81
Oatmeal	1 cup	31
Grits	1 cup	31
Cream of wheat	1 cup	28
NUTS		
Almond	1 ounce	6
Brazil nuts	1 ounce	4
Cashew,		
dry roasted with salt	1 ounce	9
Coconut, dried	1 ounce	6
Hazel nuts	1 ounce	5
Macadamia,		
dry roasted with salt	1 ounce	4
Peanuts,		
dry roasted with salt	1 ounce	7
Peanut butter, smooth	1 ounce	3
chunky	1 tbsp.	3
Pecans	1 ounce	4
Pinenuts	1 ounce	4
Pistachio,		
dry roasted with salt	1 ounce	8
Walnuts	1 ounce	4

	MEASUREMENT	GRAMS OF CARBOHYDRATE
SNACKS		
Chili con carne	1 cup	24
Pizza with cheese	1 slice	20
Burrito with meat	1	33
Veggie	1	27
Caviar on toast, 2" square	1	3
Cheeseburger	1	38
Cocktail sausage	1	1
Hamburger	1	34
Coleslaw	1 cup	16
Nachos with cheese	8 nachos	36
Submarine sandwich		
with cold cuts	1 sandwich	51
Taco	1 taco	27
Onion rings	9 rings	31
Fish filet		
breaded and battered	1 filet	15
Corn chips	1 ounce	16
Macaroni & cheese	1 cup	29
Pateé de foie gras	1 tbsp.	trace
Potato chips	1 ounce	14
Pretzels	10 pretzels	48
Chex mix	1 ounce	18
Beef jerky	1 piece	2
Granola bar	1 bar	18
Guacamole	½ cup	7
Salsa	1 ounce	1
Olives	12 olives	1
Pickle	1 pickle	3
Popcorn	1 cup	6
Trail mix	1 cup	66
Soups		
split pea with ham	1 cup	27
bouillon	1 cup	2
chicken noodle	1 cup	17
chicken rice	1 cup	7.1
New England		
clam chowder	1 cup	17
cream of chicken	1 cup	15
cream of mushroom	1 cup	9
minestrone	1 cup	11
tomato	1 cup	17
Miso	1 cup	19
SUGARS AND SWEETS		
Cakes		
Angel food	1 piece	16
Chocolate	1 piece	51
Coffee	1 piece	29
Cupcake		
with cream filling	1 cake	31
Danish pastry	1 danish	26

	MEASUREMENT	GRAMS OF CARBOHYDRATE
Doughnut, plain	1	23
glazed	1	27
Éclair	1	24
Fruit	1 piece	26
Gingerbread	1 piece	36
Pound	1 piece	14
Short	1 piece	32
Sponge	1 piece	18
Candy		
Butterfinger	1 bar	14
Fudge, chocolate		
with nuts	1 piece	13
Jelly beans	10 beans	26
M&M's, plain	10 pieces	5
peanuts	10 pieces	12
Milky Way	1 bar	47
Snickers	1 bar	34
Marshmallows	1 cup	41
Milk chocolate	1 bar	26
Cookies		
Brownies	1 bar	36
Chocolate chip	1 cookie	7
Fig bars	1 bar	11
Oatmeal	1 cookie	17
Sugar	1 cookie	10
Peanut butter	1 cookie	9
Ice cream		
vanilla	1 cup	31
chocolate	1 cup	37
frozen yogurt	½ cup	17
Jams and preserves	1 tbsp	14
Jellies	1 tbsp.	13
Molasses	1 tbsp.	12
Muffins		
blueberry	1 muffin	27
corn	1 muffin	29
oat bran	1 muffin	28
Pies		
apple	1 slice	58
cherry	1 slice	47
Lemon meringue	1 slice	53
mince meat	1 slice	62
pecan	1 slice	65
pumpkin	1 slice	30
Sugars		
granulated	1 tsp.	4
brown	1 tsp.	3
Syrup, maple	1 tbsp.	13
Table, blends Pancake	1 tbsp.	15
Chocolate	1 tbsp.	12

	MEASUREMENT	GRAMS OF CARBOHYDRATE			MEASUREMENT	GRAMS OF CARBOHYDRATE
JUICES				Tea	6 fluid oz.	trace
Apple	1 cup	29		Iced	8 fluid oz.	22
Carrot	1 cup	22				
Cranberry	1 cup	36		**ALCOHOLIC BEVERAGES**		
Fruit punch	1 cup	30		Beer	12 fluid oz.	13
Grape	1 cup	38		Light	12 fluid oz.	5
Grapefruit	1 cup	22		Red wine		
Lemon	1 tbsp.	trace		Cabernet	4 fluid oz.	trace
Lemonade, frozen	1 cup	26		Pinot noir	4 fluid oz.	trace
Lime	1 tbsp.	1		Merlot	4 fluid oz.	trace
Orange	1 cup	26		Burgundy	4 fluid oz.	trace
Peach	1 cup	29		Zinfandel	4 fluid oz.	trace
Pear	1 cup	32		Chianti	4 fluid oz.	trace
Pineapple	1 cup	34		White wine	4 fluid oz.	trace
Prune	1 cup	45		Chardonnay	4 fluid oz.	trace
Tangerine	1 cup	30		Sauvignon blanc	4 fluid oz.	trace
Tomato	1 cup	10		Pinot gregio	4 fluid oz.	trace
				Geverttaminaner	4 fluid oz.	trace
SALAD DRESSINGS/ SAUCES				Wine, sweet white	4 fluid oz.	5
Bleu, Roquefort	1 tbsp.	1		Fortified wines		
French	1 tbsp	3		Sherry, dry	2 fluid oz.	1
Low- fat	1 tbsp	4		Port	2 fluid oz.	7
Oil & Vinegar	1 tbsp.	trace		Vermouth, dry	3 fluid oz.	4
Italian	1 tbsp	2		sweet	3 fluid oz.	14
Low fat	1 tbsp.	trace		Champagne	4 fluid oz.	2
Mayonnaise	1 tbsp.	1		Distilled spirits;		
Ranch	1 tbsp.	3		gin, vodka, rum,		
Russian	1 tbsp.	2		brandy,and whisky	2 fluid oz.	0
Low-fat	1 tbsp.	5		Tequila	2 fluid oz.	0
Thousand island	1 tbsp.	2		Cocktails		
Low-fat	1 tbsp.	2		Irish coffee		12
BBQ sauce	tbsp.	2		Martini		0
Cheese sauce	cup	4		Bloody Mary		3
Marinara sauce	1 cup	trace		Mint Julep		3
Hot sauce	1 tsp.	trace		Old Fashioned		4
Pickle relish	1 tbsp.	5		Bullshot		4
Teriyaki sauce	1 tbsp.	3		Daiquiri		5
Vinegar	1 tbsp.	1		Seven and seven		6
				Manhattan		7
BEVERAGES				Gin and tonic		9
Club soda	12 fluid oz.	0		Tom Collins		9
Cola	12 fluid oz.	34		John Collins		9
Ginger ale	12 fluid oz.	32		Gin fizz		9
Diet cola	12 fluid oz.	0		Crème de menthe		6
Tonic	12 fluid oz.	0				
Chocolate milk	8 fluid oz.	31				
Coffee	6 fluid oz.	trace				
Egg nog	8 fluid oz.	34				
Espresso	2 fluid oz.	trace				
Milk shake						
Chocolate	11 fluid oz.	63				
Vanilla	11 fluid oz.	56				

INDEX